Adventures in Wild Canada

ADVENTURES IN
Wild Canada
JOHN AND JANET FOSTER

To John and Cathy

John Foster

Janet Foster

McClelland and Stewart

McClelland and Stewart Limited
The Canadian Publishers
25 Hollinger Road
Toronto, Ontario
M4B 3G2

CANADIAN CATALOGUING IN PUBLICATION DATA

Foster, John, 1933-
   Adventures in Wild Canada

ISBN 0-7710-3191-2

1. Natural history — Canada. I. Foster, Janet, 1940-
II. Title

QH106.F67 1984   574.971   C84-098270-4

PHOTOGRAPH CREDITS
John Foster, 1, 2, 19, 22, 26, 27, 28, 37, 42, 44, 46, 50 (below), 62, 65, 66, 67, 68, 69, 70, 73, 76, 77, 79, 94, 98, 102, 103, 104, 105, 109, 113 (above), 114, 118 (above), 119, 120, 125, 126, 134, 135 (above), 136, 137, 139, 142, 153; Janet Foster, 6, 18, 20, 23, 24, 25, 29, 30, 36, 38, 39, 40, 50 (above), 57, 71, 72, 75, 78, 80, 85, 86, 95, 100, 101, 113 (below), 118 (below), 121, 122, 123, 124, 133, 135 (below), 138, 141, 143, 144, 149; John Wilson, 11, 40; Dan Gibson, 63; Robert Ryan, 106.

DESIGN: Brant Cowie/Artplus
MAPS AND DRAWINGS: Vicki Land
TYPESETTING: Q Composition Inc.
PRINTING AND BINDING: in Hong Kong by Scanner Art Services Inc., Toronto

Black and white photographs converted from Kodachrome transparencies by Henry Yee, Toronto

Printed and bound in Hong Kong

CONTENTS

Our book is dedicated to Janet's father, Dr. John J. Green — physicist, pilot, research aeronautical engineer, and a constant wellspring of ideas and inspiration

FOREWORD

THIS PLANET IS, as far as we know, the richest banquet of sights, sounds, and smells in the universe. It is the fabulous variety represented by our human heritage and our natural heritage that produces this richness. Our human heritage seems to be rapidly dissolving into an instant pudding monoculture, but our natural heritage, however threatened, is still more varied and complex than we can comprehend. There is a part of the planet where the natural world totally dominates the landscape. Canada is composed of vast tracts of land which look much as they did thousands of years ago. These tracts are not in the south or central part of the country, but along its edges — the far north, the north-east, and the north-west. For thousands of years, man's main goal has been to make the natural world more suitable and convenient to him. He has succeeded very well almost everywhere. There are roads, villages, and cities. But if you visit the remote edges of Canada, you must do it on Nature's terms. You are very much a visitor.

Some of us crave the pleasures of visiting Nature on her own terms, of experiencing the sights, sounds, smells, and feel of this primeval environment. This is not easy to do. It takes time and effort as well as skills that many of us do not possess. John and Janet Foster are privileged. But they have created that privilege.

With their desire, determination, and skill, they have reached out to those beautiful and difficult corners of Canada. Many of these areas have been visited by only a handful of others. Most of us will never have this privilege, but luckily we can go there vicariously with John and Janet because of their skills as photographers and communicators.

My goals have always been very close to those of John and Janet. As a youngster in Toronto, I was fortunate to live on a ravine with an unpolluted stream harbouring tadpoles, minnows, and painted turtles. (It is now a storm sewer.) I could half close my eyes, look at the giant willows and grape canopies and listen to the birds, and imagine that ravine before man came to manage it. In my late teens, my summer work was as a Joe-boy at the wildlife research station in Algonquin Park. A few strokes of the paddle put me in touch with life as it had been for thousands of years in the boreal forest. As I sat on a rock and painted, I felt as if I was part of the landscape. The wildlife carried on their activities around me as if I didn't exist. I took geography at university in hopes of getting summer jobs in areas too remote to visit on my own. I had three successful summers, one in Newfoundland and two in the Arctic. In Ungava, we were four geologists and two Inuit. We tramped on tundra that our Inuit helpers thought had never been walked on by man. We named lakes and waterfalls. The arctic life cycle was at its peak. There were ten rough-legged hawk nests within an hour's hike of camp, a gyrfalcon's nest, and a golden eagle's nest. I had never worked so hard and I had never been so thrilled in all of my life.

As an artist and naturalist, I am interested in all aspects of the natural world, even my own backyard. But my greatest excitement still comes from the wild and remote places of our planet. I, too, have been privileged. I have been to some of the places that the Fosters have shown us. I am able to relive through their pictures and words the rich tapestry these areas offer. But they have also taken me to places that I will likely never be able to visit. I can share their sense of wonder at the unfathomable variety of the outer rim of Canada.

Their work is a celebration.

ROBERT BATEMAN

PREFACE

IT HAS BEEN OUR GOOD FORTUNE that our work in television has made these journeys possible. Along the way we had many experiences and adventures, and it is those that we would like to share with you, and to show you — through the photographs — something of what it was like to be there. To reach the distant, wilderness edges of our land has meant a great deal to us, and for that we thank the people who sent us out and helped make it happen: Ralph Ellis and Dan Gibson for once again allowing us artistic freedom; James and Marguerite McLean for giving us so many plans from which to deviate on location; John Wilson, our intrepid cameraman, who shared both bannock and blackflies in some of the greatest picnic spots in Canada; and, of course, Norn Garriock and executives of the Canadian Broadcasting Corporation, who finally gave in to our flood of program proposals and agreed to pay the bills.

We are also grateful to a number of our friends and colleagues who read portions of the manuscript and gave us the benefit of their comments and opinions: Wally Schaber, a white water canoeist and outfitter, who guided us so expertly down the Nahanni (and was there to fish us out when we dumped); Bill Mason, an artist, film maker and kindred spirit, whose own wilderness exploits have been both a challenge and an

inspiration; Bruce Litteljohn, a teacher and nature photographer, who perhaps better than anyone else has captured the changing moods of Superior's north shore; Dr. Art Martell, who shared many of our experiences in the north Yukon; and Art and Annie Babcock, who first introduced us to the enchanted islands of the Queen Charlottes.

We also thank the others who checked our facts and picked us up on so many important details: Monte Hummel, Dr. David Gray, Dr. Derek Ford, Dr. Nick Gessler, Dr. Tom Smith, Dr. Jon Lien and George Hobson. Any errors still remaining in the text we must claim as our own.

And finally, for keeping track of our words and wandering thoughts, and rearranging our ideas so that they made sense, we owe a very special thanks to our editor, Laurie Coulter.

CHAPTER ONE

Spring in the Misty Isles

WE WERE UNLOADING our gear at the little motel in Queen Charlotte City when another traveller, who had followed us into town from the air strip, came over and asked, "Have you people just come in from the east?" We said we had. "I thought so," he laughed. "Every time a bald eagle flew overhead your truck just about went off the road."

It was a simple but penetrating observation. Those of us who live in central Canada may be blessed with quick access to the uncounted lakes and rocky splendour of the Canadian Shield, but we do not have daily contact with ocean spray or the lush growth of a coastal rain forest. Nor do we look up every day and see bald eagles passing overhead or peregrine falcons soaring above their eyries on a sea cliff. Life along the western edge of Canada is distinctly different, and nowhere is this difference so clear as on the Queen Charlotte Islands. Here the influence of the Pacific Ocean, with its constant, nourishing flow of moist air, has produced some of the most luxuriant forest growth in the country. The encircling embrace of the sea touches every plant and animal, controlling their lives, shaping their evolution, and linking them all together, inextricably, through time. Some biologists have called the Queen Charlottes the Canadian Galapagos because of the island's unique plant and animal life that has evolved in isolation from the mainland.

We had come here to make a film, scarcely believing the good luck that had brought us to a place we had wanted to visit for a long time. That night in the motel, we dug through our research material to find the special natural history study of the islands sent to us by ecologist Bristol Foster. His own love for the islands was clear in the descriptions that kept poking through the normally cool language of science. He wrote: "The landscape is a tapestry of snow peaks, green islands, and blue sea. . . . In places, wild headlands, looming sea cliffs, stacks, and caves, thunderous surf, spume, and spray are seemingly everywhere. But just as common are peaceful inlets, sheltered bays and anchorages, hidden nooks and coves."

As canoeists, we were interested in the southern part of the archipelago, the true Misty Isles, which are cradled within the long protective arm of Moresby Island. In this wonderful jig-saw puzzle of islands are narrow passages and deep bays that offer shelter from the wind and opportunities for quiet exploring. Or so it seemed on the topographical maps. In fact, the southern islands are well protected from the casual visitor, who must get past the exposed northern headlands of Moresby Island before reaching the sheltered inlets to the south. Because the wind frequently blows at gale force through Hecate Strait, a sturdy ocean-going boat is needed for the trip, together with a thorough knowledge of the shoals and sunken rocks that lie in wait.

Our search for a boat that could carry us down to the southern islands led us to a knowledgeable and enthusiastic local couple, Art and Annie Babcock. We liked them immediately, and once we saw their boat, we knew we were going to be in good hands. Fourteen metres long, broad in the beam, and sturdily built, the *Bajo Point* looked ideal. Originally a west coast troller, it had been converted to a cruise ship available for charter. In the wheel-house were all the navigation aids necessary for these waters: depth sounders, radar, and radios on several frequencies. We would have a choice of camping ashore at night or sleeping on board. As a result of some creative carpentry, the boat could sleep several people quite comfortably.

Three days after our arrival, we were sailing east and south from Graham Island, moving to the soft, rhythmic thumping of the old diesel engine. Art and Annie usually take small groups of tourists and naturalists down among the islands; this time, their boat was jammed with packs, camera cases, and dive gear. On the roof of the cabin was a fibreglass canoe and an inflatable Zodiac, while Art's little skiff trailed astern. The smaller craft would be needed for exploring shallow inlets, for going ashore, and for running in close to land where reefs and sand-bars lurk. On our ten-day voyage, we hoped to film sea lions, peregrines, hotsprings, historic Haida village sites, and rain forests. And we also hoped for a mixture of weather in order to capture the special qualities of light and mist that are so distinctive in the Queen Charlotte Islands. However, after a few days we wished that Nature would be a little less co-operative in providing us with mist and rain!

Wednesday, May 10	Cloudy, with some rain, then gale force winds and heavy rain.
Thursday, May 11	Some cloud, then sun, then rain again.
Friday, May 12	Rain all night, mostly rain all day.
Saturday, May 13	Mostly rain. Very grey, no redeeming virtues.

In spite of the weather, we made several trips ashore by canoe, camping along beaches or under the shelter of great cedars, and filming in the rain when necessary. Rain is a reality in the Charlottes; the towering forest would not exist without it. When the clouds did clear away and the sun burned off the mist, we were almost disappointed. The islands were pretty and the sea a sparkling blue, but that special quality was indeed missing. The most breathtaking scenes occurred when mist and low clouds were pierced here and there by sunlight, giving them a brightness that contrasted with the warm greens of the hills. Sometimes we had to be quick to capture a certain effect before it was gone — a momentary shaft of light, or a glint on the water that suddenly breathed life into a scene.

The *Bajo Point* cruised slowly southward, squeezing through narrow channels and tiptoeing over shoals as it probed deeper among the islands. In the shallow bays where the depth sounder ticked off a rapid warning, we took to the canoe and drifted quietly on the clear salt water, looking down at the vivid colours and assorted shapes of sea stars, urchins and sea cucumbers, the long tendrils of kelp, and other animal and plant life on the bottom. The canoe was in its element — able to whisper closely along the shore under lofty trees and soaring cliffs. Once we circled an almost vertical island where, high above us, a pair of peregrines cried anxiously from a gnarled old cedar leaning over the precipice. This was their home; their eggs or young lay concealed somewhere on the ledge, protected by the sheer rock that only a professional climber could scale.

The Queen Charlotte Islands are one of the last great strongholds of the peregrine falcon in North America. Although populations are inching upward in some of the other traditional ranges, among the islands the falcons have flourished. Isolation, a plentiful diet of sea birds, and excellent nesting sites on lonely cliffs have made life easier here than elsewhere for these sensitive birds. In fact, the Queen Charlotte peregrine is the largest of its kind, a subspecies known as the Peale's peregrine.

Unfortunately, illegal trade among unscrupulous falconers has led to the theft of both eggs and young birds from eyries in the Charlottes, and now the local pilots keep a sharp look-out for suspicious boats and aircraft — a discovery we made very quickly. While we were circling the island, a single-engined airplane, en route from a lumber camp to Queen Charlotte City, swung over and had a look at us. Uncertain of our intentions, and knowing that this was an island with peregrines, the pilot immediately reported our presence to a conservation officer. We did not find out about this until our return, but when we did, we were pleased and impressed to learn that the local pilots cared about these rare and protected birds.

After four days, the weather began to improve, and we made plans to camp for a night on Hotsprings Island. In the warm shelter of a quiet bay, Art swung the canoe over the side with the boat's winch and lowered it carefully to the water. We dropped in packs

and camera gear, climbed over the side, and paddled toward a beach near the springs that give the island its name. Art had assured us that we would be able to take a bath there — a pleasant prospect after four days of cruising in generally wet weather — but we were astonished when we discovered the full meaning of his promise.

Janet made the discovery first. She was out of the canoe and off to explore as soon as the bow slid up on the sand. As I was carrying packs up the beach in search of a campsite, I heard a delighted whoop from the bushes. There, in a clearing surrounded by wild flowering shrubs, stood a white, cast-iron bathtub full of steaming hot water, which poured in from a pipe at one end and overflowed from the tub at the other. Hot springs indeed. But where had the tub come from?

The story began some years earlier. Haida fishermen, who were probably cold and stiff after too many days at sea, went ashore on Hotsprings Island with the intention of arranging hot baths for the future. It was an ideal location. No one lived on the island, and the springs flowed year-round in shallow rivulets to the sea. But the streams were too shallow for a satisfying dip, and so, manhandling not one but two old, heavy bathtubs, the fishermen struggled up the sloping shore to just below the springs. Once the tubs were in place, the men went to work with long lengths of plastic hose between the springs and the tubs. In no time at all, they were luxuriating in hot baths. One tub even features two inlet pipes — from two different springs — offering a choice of warm or very hot water. The trick, as I soon found out, was to blend the flow from the two pipes.

It was too good to be true. On this deserted island, under clear skies, with splendid views all around, we lay day-dreaming in tubs of steamy water — water that was coming to us from deep within the earth, its source of heat the volcanic rock far below. Off shore, the *Bajo Point* cruised slowly back and forth. Suddenly there was a flash of movement, a moment of graceful perfection in the sky above us. A single peregrine falcon soared and swooped and climbed, expressing its freedom, a symbol of the isolation of these wild islands. It was also, without question, the first peregrine we had ever seen while taking a bath!

Perhaps the bathtubs are an intrusion in such wilderness, yet in their own way they represent a fragment of human history — the ingenious solution by hard-working fishermen to the discomfort of cold, wet days at sea. But while the tubs are a touch of recent history, the real story of the occupation of these islands goes back many thousands of years, for this was — and still is — the land of the Haida.

Two days earlier, on an island to the north, we had seen the mossy remains of immense old timbers and the faint outlines on the forest floor of what were once superbly constructed lodges. Hand-hewn cedar logs, carefully mortised together, stood weathering in the dark forest. Only silence prevailed now over sites that had known laughter and the vibrant activity of community life. Where there had been clearings, houses, totem-poles, and dug-out canoes, there was wilderness once more. The signs that were left, though, gave us a tantalizing glimpse of a people whose traditions reach back at least 8000 years.

The Haida were blessed with plentiful marine and woodland resources and a benign climate. Long before the first Europeans sailed to the Queen Charlottes, the Haida were living in comfortable lodges and structuring their lives within an organized social fabric. They were master builders and artists, and highly competent on both land and sea. At the centre of their culture stood the giant cedar, straight and strong and easy to carve, with soft bark that could be used in dozens of practical and decorative ways. It is quite probable that when the Haida were first contacted by Spaniards from Mexico or Spain in 1774, they had developed a social and cultural structure which surprised the explorers, who gazed in astonishment at the massive yet graceful canoes that came out to meet them. One historian estimates that their longest canoes, each carved from the trunk of a single cedar, could carry forty people and almost two tonnes of supplies.

Inevitably, contact with the outside world changed their world. At first, the trading of sea otter pelts for woodworking tools and other useful European goods brought cultural advances, and the Haida flourished as never before. However, in the long run, the invasion of profit-seeking traders carried with it the seeds of failure for the original Haida culture and lifestyle. When diseases introduced by explorers, settlers, and workers swept the islands, decimating the population, the old villages began to empty. The forest moved rapidly over the deserted lodges, reclaiming the land.

Archaeology on the islands has barely begun; many of the villages are still awaiting rediscovery. In a few places, grey and weathered totem-poles still stand, messengers from the past glory of Haida culture. We also heard tales of huge cedar canoes that had been found in the forest, and no doubt there will be more exciting discoveries to come, as archaeologists explore the forest or, ironically, as loggers cut it down.

Today, most of the residents of the Queen Charlotte Islands, including the direct descendants of the original Haida, live on Graham Island. South Moresby is populated mostly by isolated communities of loggers, who live in large temporary camps. Deep concern attends the advance of the chain-saws into these pristine southern islands — a concern shared by the Haida, who fear the ecological disruption that comes with clear cutting and the resulting damage to their traditional food gathering areas. This concern has grown with the Haida people's resurgence of pride in their history and culture. Many now have world-class reputations as artisans; their carvings and fine jewellery are eagerly sought by collectors. Some have begun carving the giant cedars once more, and others are building finely crafted houses in the style of their ancestors. Their link with the forest is being forged again; this is still their home.

On our way south we had passed close to the site of an old Haida settlement called Skedans. Poor weather had discouraged us from going ashore; instead, we had ducked in behind Louise Island for shelter and sailed down to our present location at Hotsprings Island. But now the sea was calm, and when we arrived back on board the *Bajo Point* after our hot baths and a pleasant night on the beach, Art and Annie had a suggestion for us: "How would you like to visit Skedans and also film a northern sea lion colony?" Inside the wheel-house, Art picked up a chart and pointed to a rocky headland. "The sea lions haul out there in the summer," he said. "It's not a breeding colony, just a place where they rest and go fishing. There's a little bay behind the headland, and if you take the canoe in there, you can go ashore and climb the rocks behind the sea lions."

After we had laid out a course and turned north, we began to discuss the possibility of getting some underwater footage of the colony. John Wilson, our friend and cameraman, had brought his dive gear, and we had several tanks of compressed air on board. Art,

who also dives, could suit up and stand by as safety man. John was convinced the sea lions would not attack him, although other divers are less certain. He had dived with these huge mammals before, off the Valdes Peninsula of Patagonia. Any fear he might have felt — and he showed none as usual — was overcome by his irrepressible enthusiasm and the confidence of years of experience filming wildlife behaviour. Soon he was tugging on his wet suit, checking the regulator, and preparing his electric Beaulieu camera in its clear plastic housing. With a full magazine, he would have about five-and-a-half minutes of actual filming time before having to surface to reload.

About a kilometre from the sea lions' rocky point, we hove to and considered an approach that would not disturb the colony. As quietly as possible, John and Art motored off in the skiff, making a wide circuit until they were out of sight of the sea lions in a little bay. From here, John planned to swim back to the point. It was a good plan and, as it turned out, the sea lions were incredibly curious. The moment that John swam into view on the surface they surrounded him, swimming a cautious fifteen metres away and constantly snorting and growling to one another. Like spectators at a golf match, they stayed with him, moving when he moved but always keeping a polite distance. Then John dived, and they all followed.

Holding the now weightless camera out in front, John slowly flippered down in about six metres of water. For a few minutes the sea lions circled warily, unsure of this lanky, black-suited, bubbling figure who had entered their world. But soon an extraordinary underwater ballet began. From all sides, the sea lions glided toward the diver. Cautiously at first, then boldly, they swooped and pirouetted around him. Some swam playfully up to the camera and nuzzled

ABOVE   *Looking west, toward South Moresby, from Titul Island.*

RIGHT   *Moisture-laden clouds build over the mountainous spine of South Moresby Island.*

the housing; others even nibbled at his flippers. With their dark, shining eyes gazing at him, John had the distinct impression that he was being courted by a few of the young females — not a very scientific interpretation, perhaps, but inescapable under the circumstances. Thus, he felt a little uneasy when a battle-scarred bull joined in and started cruising around in ominous circles. "I thought he was jealous," John said, "so I sank to the bottom and sat down with my back against a big rock." From there he continued filming.

Meanwhile, we had crept up behind the colony and were filming from the rocks above the sea lions. When John surfaced and headed back toward the skiff, we held our breath as he passed directly under another immense bull perched on the rocks above. This one appeared to be thinking about diving in on top of him. It glared down, snorting loudly at the yellow air tank. No doubt the sudden arrival in his vicinity of a two tonne, belligerent sea lion would have given John a wilderness experience to remember; however, we were relieved when the moment passed and he was safely back on board the *Bajo Point*. Weeks later, his film footage would be edited to music, in a tribute to the fluid ballet of these wild sea mammals.

The Haida site at Skedans was a sad place, with its scattered remnants of old timbers and totem-poles poking through the grasses and brush. Our sense of sadness was perhaps heightened by the knowledge that the island here had been logged right to the beach, somehow dishonouring the village and its history. It was a blunt reminder of the impact of logging on these beautiful islands.

Two hundred years or so have passed since the first explorers began to haul away profitable loads of sea otter pelts. By the late 1800s, when the search for

Art and Annie Babcock, skippers of the Bajo Point.

quick profit had turned to the forest, temporary rights were being granted for cutting high-quality virgin timber. Now the search has reached the only surviving commercial stands of original forest in the unspoiled southern islands. The rest are gone. Understandably, nothing polarizes opinion so quickly as the question of logging these last stands of virgin rain forest.

Concern has focussed on an ancient, misty watershed on Lyell Island with the evocative name of Windy Bay. This was our destination as we turned south once more. The wind was up, and rain was hammering on the roof of the cosy cabin as the *Bajo Point* rose and plunged in the swells rolling in from Hecate Strait. Sipping mint tea (it's said to be good for sea-sickness), we listened as Art and Annie described the rich and timeless qualities of Windy Bay, with its salmon streams and almost tropical rain forest. Here, they told us, was the last significant and still forested watershed of any size on the east side of the Queen Charlottes. Its profusion of wildlife includes the most productive salmon stream in the South Moresby Island area. Pink salmon, coho salmon, rainbow trout, cut-throat trout, and Dolly Varden can be seen in Windy Bay Creek and its estuary, particularly during the spawning runs in autumn. At this time, Art told us, you can walk beside the streams and spot bald eagles by the dozen and black bears — all gathered to feast on salmon in the shallows. Along the shoreline to the north live enormous sea bird colonies, including the largest known colonies of ancient murrelets in Canada. These swift little birds nest on the ground beneath the trees in the forest. Two peregrine falcon eyries were also on the Babcocks' list of natural resources. Lastly, they described two old village sites and evidence of early forest utilization by the Haida.

Throughout this watershed, the connections between wildlife and forest are direct and vital. One perfect example is the link between the Peale's peregrine, the ancient murrelet, and the forest. The large peregrine depends for most of its diet upon the small murrelet. It, in turn, depends upon an undisturbed forest floor for its nesting habitat. It is interrelationships like these — the bonding of land and sea and wild creatures, the links between animal and forest — that are so easily cut with a chain-saw.

Windy Bay's green hilltops were lost in the mist as we cruised carefully toward the shallow mouth of Windy Bay Creek. Art decided to take us ashore in the Zodiac, while Annie held the *Bajo Point* out in the safety of deep water. As we entered the estuary, the forest seemed to close in around us. The rain had stopped and moisture dripped from ancient trees draped with the trailing arms of mosses and ferns. Soon the almost tropical forest of cedar, spruce, hemlock, and cypress towered over us, and we left the Zodiac to explore an awesome, silent world. Our feet sank into spongy mosses as we slowly made our way through the crumbling debris of giant cedars that had died and fallen ages ago and were now returning to the earth. Fifty or sixty metres above us, the canopy almost closed out the sky, allowing only a soft, dim light to reach the forest floor. In fact, it was so dark in these tangled glades that we could not film; our light meters barely flickered. And then it began to rain again.

All day we waited for the sky to brighten, and each time we entered the forest, encouraged by a few shafts of sunlight, it started to rain. Perhaps this was to be expected in a rain forest, but what we wanted were bright, hazy conditions that would cast a warm, shadow-free light among the trees. Direct sunlight would create a new problem; there would be so much contrast between the rays of light and the deeper shadows that the image on film would be very busy and confusing. Yet the tiny ferns, cobwebs, and mosses needed a touch of sunlight to show their graceful designs. Shadow-free light for the wide shots and direct sunlight for the fine detail would have been perfect. During those moments when our meters did detect enough light, we quickly learned to put ourselves into the scene before the camera. Only with a human figure in the picture could the camera reveal the true size and scale of these soaring trees. On our farm in southern Ontario, a cedar is considered large if it is more than thirty centimetres across. Here they were as wide as our cabin.

Such is the forest of Windy Bay. Like an ancient civilization, it speaks to us of the history of our land. It seemed unthinkable to us that anyone could allow this watershed to be stripped of its trees. The old analogy came to mind: standing in the forest of Windy Bay was like standing in a historic, priceless cathedral. However, this place did have a price on it. Profits

ABOVE   *Giant cedars of the original rain forest stood at the heart of the Haida culture and now stand at the heart of the controversy over the logging of these islands.*

RIGHT   *Our camp on Hotsprings Island, with a view across to South Moresby Island.*

ABOVE *A weathered totem-pole on Anthony Island. To-day, the Skidegate Band Council offers guided tours of ancient historic sites in the Queen Charlottes.*

LEFT *The finest remaining group of totem-poles on the islands stands at Ninstints on Anthony Island. This ancestral home of the Haida is now a World Heritage Site.*

could be made, at least for the short term. But in the long run, in terms of its value to this generation and all those to come, there could be no question; Windy Bay is valuable beyond calculation. I thought of the words of Bill Reid, an island resident, who wrote: "What is happening on the poor old Charlottes resembles the desperate efforts of a band of brigands intent on looting a treasure house before the owners realize what's going on and take measures to stop it — this on our famous Misty Isles, home of the fabled Haida, one of the places in our country still imbued with romance, a world-renowned, unique ecological area."

Windy Bay represents just one watershed. In a world where forests are disappearing at a rate of 2000 hectares an hour, it seems reasonable enough to ask that one complete watershed be set aside. But the lumber companies have fought hard to reduce the size of the proposed ecological reserve. The struggle to save Windy Bay has been another of those desperate rearguard actions in the field of conservation — a last stand among 500-year-old trees. The trouble is that coastal logging practices here are devastating; steep hillsides are stripped, and logging roads are gashed back and forth across the slopes. Heavy rains do the rest. They dislodge the thin soils and their web of organic matter from the smooth rock underneath, starting landslides that carry tonnes of debris down into the precious spawning gravels of salmon streams, and down to the beaches and sea bird colonies — a heavy price to pay for some short-term gain. The short-term gain here has been estimated as equivalent to the proceeds of about five days of province-wide logging in British Columbia.

That night we sat in the warm glow of the lights in the *Bajo Point*'s cabin and discussed the future of

Evidence of a long-abandoned Haida village, now overtaken by the forest.

ABOVE   *Steam rising from the springs on Hotsprings Island.*

LEFT   *A perfect way to warm up after a few rainy days at sea. The old tub is fed by water diverted from the hotsprings.*

A colony of northern sea lions on the stormy southern tip of the Queen Charlottes.

A Peale's peregrine falcon, a wild symbol of the Queen Charlotte Islands.

the islands. For a long time we wrestled with a question that is becoming all too familiar. How much publicity can a wild area endure before its sudden fame brings new pressures? If public outcry saved Windy Bay from the chain-saws, would that same public flock to these southern islands in such numbers that the area would be changed forever? Yet to do nothing would indicate acceptance of the argument that forests are best turned into lumber and jobs. Windy Bay would become another licenced tree farm. No, Windy Bay had to be exposed to public attention. Our own visit and the film we were making were one small part of that process.

Next morning, the Babcocks anchored the *Bajo Point* off the isolated sand beach of Woodruff Bay, close to the tip of the Charlottes. Long, low swells were running in from the south, a sure sign that we were moving out of the protection of the islands and getting closer to the open sea. Art lowered the canoe over the side again, and Janet and I paddled toward the shore. Waves were crashing on the beach, making a dry landing impossible, but we could see a protected cove behind a reef and knew we could go ashore there.

The day was overcast and quiet; only the hiss and splash of waves along the beach broke the silence. Then just as we slid in behind the protection of the reef, a huge, barnacle-crusted body rose a few paddle strokes away, expelled a mighty burst of air, inhaled again, and sank below the surface. Although we had had time only for a glimpse, it was, without question, a grey whale. Paddles flailing, we shot over to where the water still boiled. I reached for a camera. The whale must have been feeding in the shallows, but would it surface again? Could we get close to it in the canoe? For long moments we drifted and waited,

A huge bull sea lion poised above our cameraman, John Wilson, who snorkels by completely unaware of it.

but the whale had gone. We headed once more toward the shore.

The prize on any west coast or off-shore island beach is a Japanese glass float that has bobbed across the Pacific and rolled ashore on the sand. Some are as big as basketballs, others are quite small. Janet, racing ahead as usual, soon gave a triumphant yell, dropped to her knees, and came up clutching a tiny blue glass sphere. It had been tucked away in some dried kelp at the high-water mark. Her prize, which may have been drifting at sea for years, must have found its way here on the warm Japanese Current that circles endlessly past these shores, bringing with it the moist winds, the rain, and the temperate climate.

The Bajo Point, a west coast troller that has been converted into a comfortable cruise ship.

Gathering up some driftwood, we made a small fire for toasting sandwiches and talked about the experiences of the past ten days. Looking back, what had surprised us the most was the sheltered, intimate quality of the islands and the luxuriant growth extending down to the edge of the water. "I think I'll always remember stepping into the forest and seeing those old Haida ruins," Janet said. "It was like finding a lost civilization." For a while we also talked about the possibility of a canoe trip through the islands, but as we looked out into the bay at our comfortable mother ship quietly sitting at anchor, we realized that here was the best way to see the Charlottes — by boat, with side-trips by canoe whenever possible. Had we come two or three hundred years earlier, there might have been an even better way — in a long, sleek, ocean-going Haida canoe. Then perhaps we could have glimpsed life as it was for thousands of years, with the bountiful ocean on one side and a benevolent, embracing forest on the other.

CHAPTER TWO

LAND OF THE CARIBOU

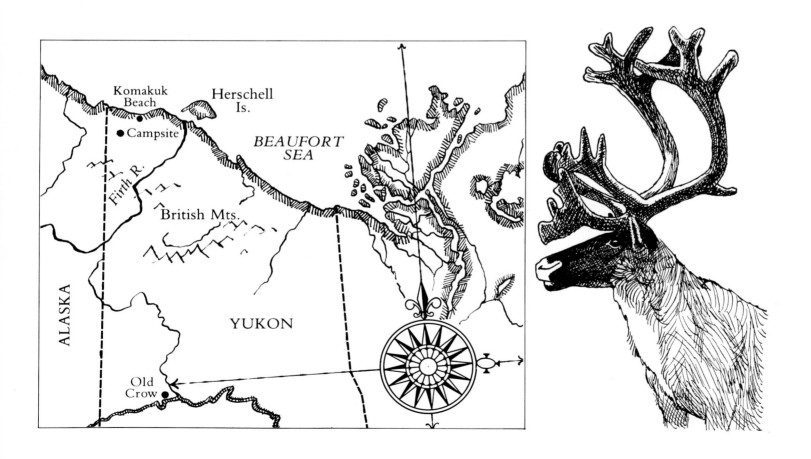

Even from a distance, the female grizzly looked awesomely large. Through our binoculars and 400 millimetre camera lenses, she appeared even larger as she worked her way toward us along the bank of a rushing stream still filled with torrents of icy meltwater. She was in no hurry. As she casually flipped over rocks and nosed among the low bushes searching for grubs, we could see the muscles rippling in her massive shoulders beneath the thick, dark fur. She moved at a leisurely pace, a powerful creature very much at ease in the arctic wilderness of the north Yukon.

Following closely behind and examining every turned rock and crevice with interest was her big, year-old cub. In contrast to its mother, the yearling was pale, almost golden in colour. Both grizzlies were absorbed in their search and completely unaware of John and me. There was little chance the bears could see us perched on a rocky hill, although contrary to popular belief, grizzlies do have good eyesight. They can recognize shapes and movement from a distance, but prefer to rely on their hearing and their highly developed sense of smell for information. I remembered one expert who claimed that a grizzly could "take a sniff of you half a mile downwind and tell you the colour of your grandmother's wedding dress." These two had not yet caught our scent, but they were drawing closer. We crouched lower among the rocks.

Grizzlies have had little contact with people on the Yukon's North Slope; few travellers visit this remote arctic landscape. And because these northern grizzlies are unaccustomed to human scent, they dislike it, finding the smell strange and unfamiliar. Generally at the first whiff, they will turn and run, or so the theory goes. Watching mother and cub steadily approaching, I had a feeling that the theory was about to be tested.

This was our first good look at a barren-ground grizzly, and after carefully noting the size of the mother's front feet, I quickly put aside any notion I had of trying to find a better, closer camera angle. As photographers, we wanted to get the best possible pictures of the bears moving freely in their own environment, unaware of our presence. Nevertheless, we knew that the sensible thing to do was to let them know we were there. We had been warned never to surprise a grizzly at close range. It was impossible to predict how this mother would react if she suddenly came upon us.

There was no safe line of retreat from our position on top of the hill, and we were afraid that any sudden movement on our part would draw the mother's attention to us. Better to remain still. As the animals wandered closer, I cast about in my mind trying to remember all that we had read and been told about proper etiquette when unexpectedly confronting a grizzly. "Move away slowly at a forty-five-degree angle so the bear can see you are leaving," advised one biologist. "If he charges you, then you charge him right back — grizzlies are nine-tenths bluff," said another. And a national park brochure recommends that if no other choices are available, "lie down on the ground with your knees under your chin, hands behind your neck, and play dead." Travellers who followed such procedures were said to have suffered "only minor injuries." What, I wondered, would be a minor injury from a grizzly bear?

I rummaged in my pack for the small flare gun. It might not be very effective against an angry grizzly, but perhaps the loud bang and the explosion of red light would be enough of a deterrent. We had brought a high-powered rifle with us on this expedition, but it was to be used only as a last resort, if we were faced with a life-threatening situation. Now John fingered the barrel nervously and reached into his pocket for the cartridge clip.

By this time, the two animals had reached a bend in the stream bed that brought them almost directly across from our look-out. The mother was ambling along with her sensitive nose held close to the ground, picking up the fragrant smells of early spring from the tundra. Suddenly she stopped, rose up high on her back legs, and took a long, deep sniff — catching our scent. The response was instantaneous. She wheeled around and clawed her way frantically up the steep bank, sending a shower of loose gravel cascading down the slope. Without so much as a pause or a backward glance, she tore out across the open tundra with her startled cub charging along behind, scarcely able to keep up. Moments later, they had become two dark specks shimmering and then disappearing into the ground haze.

It had all happened so fast. Our feeling of excitement upon seeing the grizzlies soon gave way to a sense of relief that our presence had not provoked a confrontation. Certainly we did not want to be responsible for causing the unnecessary deaths of the very creatures we had come to observe and photograph. We also felt a great sadness that this magnificent animal, one that fears nothing in the wild, should have reacted immediately and with such alarm to our scent. Where did its fear originate? Did the grizzly bear have an encounter with primitive man that somehow left an indelible imprint on its genetic memory? We could only wonder as we hiked back through the long, wide valley to our campsite.

It was early June, the beginning of arctic spring. Patches of snow still lingered on the gravelly hilltops, and down in the ravines and shaded gullies, it lay piled in wet, heavy drifts. The project that had brought us to this northern territory had begun months earlier with elaborate preparations and considerable research. We had been asked to make a film about the Yukon's North Slope and, specifically, about the Porcupine caribou herd, whose wanderings across the Barren Grounds stretch back further than human memory. There are more than 100 000 caribou in the herd. In early March, the cows leave their wintering grounds in the Yukon's forested interior to begin a journey that takes them hundreds of kilometres to their calving grounds, a huge area spanning the tundra slopes and coastal plains of the north Yukon and Alaska. They arrive in late May, and the calves are born soon after. Our plan was to put ourselves in the path of the caribou and film their migration.

Our filming location would be an unnamed valley in the far north-west corner of the Yukon, about as far north and west as you can go on Canada's mainland. The valley had been chosen for us by Dr. Art Martell, a biologist with the Canadian Wildlife Service. Art has spent many summers on the North Slope studying the caribou and making detailed notes of their numbers and movements. In particular, he has studied what vegetation they eat, how often they stop to feed, and for how long. In spring, for example, the pregnant cows require a nutritious forage that is rich in protein. From past observation, Art knew that this valley was one of several along the North Slope that had such vegetation. After studying maps and aerial photographs, and knowing the traditional migratory routes of the caribou, Art placed his bet and gambled that this year part of the herd would pass through our valley as they emerged from the foothills onto the coastal plain. "And if you're really lucky," he added, "you'll have young calves right around your camp."

But there were no guarantees. The caribou are completely unpredictable. They know any number of different routes through the mountains and foothills to the arctic coast. One year, the herd will follow one chain of valleys, the next year it will follow another. In this immense wilderness region, who can tell which route the caribou will choose? We were going to need a great deal of luck.

With our destination pin-pointed on a map, we began the larger job of planning and packing. The filming would involve five or six weeks of work, and our entire life support system had to travel with us. Into our packs went thick sleeping-bags, storm-proof tents, clothing, film gear, and even camp-stoves. There would be no firewood or shelter where we were going.

Our food was mostly freeze-dried — complete packaged meals that are light, easy to pack, and need little cooking. More importantly, they carry no strong smells to attract grizzlies into camp. All the food supplies were packed into sturdy, well-fitting plywood boxes, which John had made especially for the trip. They would be reasonably bear-proof, and at camp they could double as seats. On the subject of clothing, we consulted our autumn canoe tripping list, adding parkas, heavy sweaters, thermal underwear, and headnets. We also questioned biologists and park planners who had been to the North Slope before. They warned us to expect everything from heat-waves to blizzards, with hordes of bloodthirsty mosquitoes in-between.

Finally we were packed and on our way. Four of us were making the long journey. Our cameraman, John Wilson, and his assistant, Ross Wilson, had as much equipment as we had, maybe more. Watching it all being swallowed up by the conveyor belt at the airport, I could not help wondering how many of our packs, boxes, and camera cases would successfully make the trip. (As it turned out, one of the heavy tripods disappeared forever somewhere between Toronto and Inuvik in the Northwest Territories.) Two days later, contemplating our mountain of gear on the cold and windy air strip at Inuvik, we asked ourselves whether we had brought too much. But it was all essential, nothing could be left behind, or so we told the pilot of the Twin Otter, who was examining our luggage with a highly critical eye. Weight is an important factor in northern flying, and he made us weigh every item — and every member of our crew — before he loaded the aircraft. From that day forward, we called ourselves "the travelling ton."

Flying west from Inuvik, we began a three-hour flight over the frozen lakes, channels, and islands of

ABOVE *The grizzly bears on the Yukon's North Slope have had little contact with people, and the human scent is often unfamiliar to them.*

LEFT *Look closely at the lower left-hand corner of the photograph. Those little dots are our tents, perched on a plateau and almost lost amid the vastness of the North Slope foothills.*

ABOVE   *This young arctic ground squirrel was frequently in John Wilson's tent, rummaging about for granola.*

RIGHT   *At two o'clock in the morning, angry storm clouds moved into the mountains and left our valley bathed in sunlight. A telephoto lens isolates one of the distant peaks.*

The front vestibule of this tent came in handy for sitting out a three-day storm.

the Mackenzie Delta, and up along the arctic coast to a radar base at Komakuk Beach called Bar One. The station, situated at the edge of the Beaufort Sea not far from the Alaskan border, is part of North America's Distant Early Warning Line. As we circled and came in for a landing on the gravel air strip, John remarked that the radar complex — with its narrow, low building, its huge rectangular dishes pointing northward, and its radome gleaming like a giant golf ball — looked like an abandoned set from an old science fiction movie. For us, however, it was a tiny outpost of civilization, a final step before heading into the interior.

At Komakuk Beach, we discussed our project with John Russell, a Yukon Game Branch biologist involved in a study of the caribou migration. He would be spending many hours in a spotter airplane, tracking and counting the caribou as they moved out of the foothills and along the coastal plain into Alaska. John also volunteered to be our "eyes in the sky." From time to time, if we were able to establish radio contact, he would bring us word when the caribou were approaching our valley.

We were soon ready to begin the last leg of our journey. John and I would make the trip to our campsite first, followed by John Wilson and Ross. Parks Canada had a Jet Ranger helicopter working in the area where we would be filming and had generously agreed to help move us around this remote land. Next day, John and I lifted off noisily from Komakuk Beach in the chopper and skimmed out across the flat coastal plain toward the British Mountains. Now we had our first look at the Yukon's North Slope, a vast wilderness of mountain ranges, tundra meadows, powerful rivers, sparkling bogs, and winding valleys. It is a land that has existed virtually unchanged through

thousands of years. This part of North America escaped the last great ice sheet, which buried and altered the physical features of much of the continent. It became a refuge for plants, animals, and early man. In many ways, the north Yukon is a window looking into the past, for evidence can be found here of the flora and fauna that thrived 40 000 years ago.

At one time, a land bridge joined Asia to North America over what is now the Bering Sea. A host of strange Asian animals found their way across it into Alaska and the Yukon. There were woolly mammoths, sabre-toothed tigers, mastodons, lions, giant beavers, camels — and there were caribou. Walled off from the rest of the continent for many years by the great glacial barriers, these creatures made the grasslands of the north Yukon their home. Today, only the fossilized bones of those earlier giant mammals remain, but the caribou are still here, still following their ancient migratory routes across the North Slope. Used for hundreds and hundreds of years, their trails have become permanent pathways running like dark veins through the valleys, up across the scree slopes, and over the hilltops.

The North Slope is vitally important to the Porcupine herd. Here the pregnant cows give birth to their calves, feed on the nutritious vegetation, and recover from the ordeal of migration. By summer's end, they have built up enough energy reserves to begin the journey back to their winter range. The calving grounds that span the Yukon-Alaska border make the Porcupine herd a truly international resource. On the Alaskan side, an Arctic National Wildlife Range has already been created to protect the calving grounds, and in 1978 the Canadian Government prohibited any further oil exploration or development on the North Slope. At the time, it was understood that

part of that land was to be set aside as a national park, but long-term protection for the entire area — and for the caribou — is still by no means assured.

Even if the caribou were not here, the North Slope would fit all the criteria for a superb arctic park. The same range that is so well suited to the Porcupine herd also supports a rich variety of other wildlife species. Dall's sheep roam the Richardson Mountains and along the banks of the Firth River, arctic foxes den along the braided river deltas near the coast, and barren-ground grizzlies find in this remote wilderness the isolation they need from human contact and civilization. In springtime, as the uppermost layer of permafrost thaws, migrating birds begin to arrive on the coastal plain by the tens of thousands to nest among its shallow lakes and watery meadows. Their names read like a roll-call from a North American field guide: whistling swans, arctic loons, mergansers, arctic terns, pintails, oldsquaws. Still others, such as the snow geese, use the plain as a staging area before moving on to their breeding territories on the more distant arctic islands. Sandpipers, golden plovers, and lapland longspurs breed on the uplands. And among the craggy ramparts of the British Mountains, and along the high canyon walls of the Firth River, nest gyrfalcons and the rare, endangered peregrines. The Yukon's North Slope is indeed a place worthy of national park status.

Wedged tightly into the helicopter's back seat beside our packs, I peered out the small window, hoping to catch sight of caribou. But the land seemed barren and rather colourless. Nothing had turned green yet, and there was no sign of life. In front, John and the

Caribou peacefully graze the tundra meadows, putting on fat and rebuilding strength lost during calving and migration.

OPPOSITE ABOVE   *We climbed out of a dried-up stream bed to find ourselves in the middle of a caribou herd. The bulls seemed far more curious than frightened.*

OPPOSITE BELOW   *The calves follow closely behind their mothers, nose to tail, as the herd crosses the fast-moving Firth.*

RIGHT   *After struggling across the river, the herd streams up the far bank and on over the plateau with scarcely a pause or a break in stride.*

pilot had their heads bent over the topographical map, trying to match the wavy contour lines with the landscape below. Their voices crackled over my headset as they plotted our course, quickly identifying one landform after another. "There it is," John yelled back at me as we came over a hilltop and swept down into a wide valley. Running through the middle of it was a shallow, sparkling river, its banks still dotted with sheets of ice. On one side of the valley, partway up the gravelly slope, was a broad, flat plateau. It corresponded exactly with the circle that Art Martell had drawn on our map. "That's it! That's our campsite."

After circling the plateau once, we landed on a patch of level ground that was free of rocks. Scrambling out, we unloaded our gear with the noise of the Jet Ranger screaming in our ears and the wind from the rotor blades threatening to blow everything away. We stayed low, keeping well clear of the tail rotor. Moving around a live helicopter can be dangerous, even more so if it is perched on uneven ground and the blades are whirling around at head height on the upward side. We had heard too many tales of passengers leaving a helicopter and unwittingly walking into the tail rotor. Lying spread-eagled over our packs and nearly choking in the storm of dust being blown up, we held everything tightly in place and gave the thumbs-up signal to the pilot. The chopper lifted off and flew like a noisy bumble-bee back to Komakuk Beach for Ross and John Wilson.

As the sound of the helicopter faded away, we felt a sense of relief, the good feeling of having arrived at the end of a journey that had taken a long time in

The Firth River cuts across the North Slope of the Yukon. Note the caribou herd at upper left.

preparation. It was four o'clock in the afternoon. There was no hurry to set up camp — the sun would still be shining at midnight — so we took a few moments and sat at the edge of the plateau, enjoying the solitude and the silence.

From our lofty perch, we had a good view in all directions. To the north, the valley stretched to the coastal plain and the white edge of the frozen Beaufort Sea, some twenty-four kilometres away. To the south lay the steep foothills of the British Mountains, and on both sides of the valley, grey scree slopes climbed sharply upward. There were no caribou in the valley, but judging by the number of well-worn trails running across the far hillside, caribou had come this way many times in the past.

Surprisingly, the land that had seemed so bare and drab from the air was speckled with tiny, brightly coloured arctic flowers. There was a wonderful sense of space — a feeling that here you could walk across the rolling hills forever and never tire of the view, or see the end of it. There was a sense of timelessness, too. Day and night soon lose much of their meaning when the sun never sets. Before long, we stopped looking at our watches altogether and just went by our body time, sleeping when we felt tired and eating when we grew hungry. There are few places where you can experience such a complete feeling of freedom.

It was time to turn our attention to the more practical question of unpacking gear and establishing the base camp. A quick survey revealed an ideal spot for the tents down at the far tip of the plateau. The ground was relatively flat there, and a small stream gurgling by on its way down into the valley would provide a handy water supply. We began to move our packs, but suddenly heard a string of anxious cries. Running

back and forth on the tundra was a golden plover. It seemed very upset, bobbing its head up and down and calling repeatedly. As we cautiously approached, the bird tried desperately to lead us away, first in one direction, then in another. Soon a second plover arrived, and the air was filled with their distressed yet musical calls. The best campsite was already occupied!

John's sharp eyes spotted the eggs first — four of them nestled into a small depression in the tundra. They blended in so well that we would never have seen them unless we had been looking. Marking the location of the nest carefully so that we could avoid it in the future, we backed hastily away. The plateau was not large, but in the weeks to come it would be necessary to maintain a respectful distance from the nest site, at least until the eggs had hatched. As we moved down to the opposite end of the plateau, we could not help reflecting on the amusing side of the situation: the circle drawn on our maps weeks before and hundreds of kilometres away to mark our suggested campsite had accurately pin-pointed a golden plover's territory!

The first few days at camp were quiet ones as the four of us settled in, looked for camera positions, and explored our immediate surroundings. A pair of horned larks was nesting on the scree slope behind camp, and in a little gully at the edge of the plateau a male rock ptarmigan, still in his white winter plumage, strutted back and forth across his territory. His mate was somewhere close by on the nest; however, she was well camouflaged against the brown tundra, and we never did see her. There was also a large family of arctic ground squirrels whose burrows were tunnelled into the face of our plateau.

The sun was hot and the winds blew warm in the valley. Indeed, it was hard to believe we were in the

Arctic. The climate of the north Yukon is mild compared to the rest of arctic Canada; so mild, in fact, that it has been nicknamed "the banana belt." Our first three days bore out the description, but it was not to last. On the fourth day, I was down on the valley floor, kneeling between two ice floes on the river bank, trying to wash my hair in the fast-moving water. One light soaping and a quick rinse was about all that I could endure. Straightening up, I towelled my aching head furiously, trying to work some feeling back into it and my tingling fingers. And that was the moment an icy blast of frigid arctic air chose to hit me square in the middle of my back.

The warm winds had abruptly changed direction. Now they came hurtling across the frozen Beaufort Sea and into the valley from the north-west. Peering out from under the towel, I saw a line of black storm clouds racing in from Alaska. I scrambled back up the plateau, stumbling over the top just in time to see John Wilson's tent tear free from its moorings and cart-wheel away. Our own tents were still anchored, but they were showing signs of great stress. More steel spikes were needed, and while John hurriedly hammered them into the frozen permafrost to reinforce the guy ropes, I hauled everything inside, just as heavy drops of rain began to spatter down.

Over the years, John Wilson has developed fine filming instincts, and nowhere are they more evident than in the midst of a crisis. Abandoning his own flattened tent, which by now was pegged at one end but streaming out wildly in the wind, he grabbed his tripod and camera and concentrated on filming the storm and recording the chaos at camp. Meanwhile, the temperature had tumbled down close to the freezing point, and as the full fury of the storm broke over

the valley, all memory of the "banana belt" disappeared. This was the Arctic!

The storm raged for three days, alternately pelting us with rain, sleet, and heavy, wet snow. The wind blew constantly. Snug in our sleeping-bags, we watched the tent walls billow and wondered how much strain the centre pole could take before it buckled. John and I had brought two tents with us on the expedition, one for sleeping in and a slightly larger one with a small vestibule at one end for the general day-to-day living. The vestibule proved to be ideal for sitting out storms. Depending upon which direction the wind was coming from, we could zipper one side shut and sit on the other with a good view out and enough room to safely fire up the cook-stove. It was somewhat cramped, particularly when Ross and John joined us for tea, but at least we were warm and reasonably comfortable.

At times like this, we were thankful for the freeze-dried foods that needed little preparation. It was our bannock, however, that really sustained us through the storm's darker moments. We had perfected and field-tested our special recipe long before we came north. (See recipe, p. 157.) For this trip, I pre-mixed all the dry ingredients and divided the mix into thirty individual plastic bags — one bannock per bag. All we had to do at camp was blend in a cup of water and fry it up. One bannock, served with mugs of steaming hot soup and followed with a wedge of hard chocolate for dessert, made a good, satisfying lunch. And there was nothing quite like the aroma of fresh bread wafting through the tent to raise our flagging spirits.

During the height of the storm — as we lay in our tents reading, writing up the daily log, peering out the doorway, and trying not to guess how long the foul weather might last — we saw our first caribou. They wandered into our valley in small groups of four or five. Mostly they were cows and yearlings, but sometimes we would spot a young calf that had been born somewhere back among the foothills.

Caribou are incredible animals, possessing a strength and an endurance beyond our imagining. Already they had travelled hundreds of kilometres since leaving their wintering grounds in March. Along the way, they would have encountered heavy snow underfoot, blinding blizzards, ice-choked rivers, and wolves, which prey heavily on the herds. The pregnant cows lead the migration in the spring, followed a few weeks later by the bulls and older juveniles. The cows are anxious to reach the calving grounds. They lose a great deal of weight during their journey, and they are pressed onward by the urgency and demands of the new life growing within them. Even when calves are born en route, the cows cannot afford to linger long. The newborn must adapt quickly or perish. Minutes after birth, a calf is on its feet. By the second day, staying closely behind its mother, it is able to keep up with the moving herd. And on the third day, it is said that a healthy calf can outrun a grizzly bear.

It was too dark to film through the storm, so we crouched in the doorway of the tent and watched through binoculars. The caribou were almost invisible against the valley floor and seemingly oblivious to the elements raging about them. Sometimes they would stop and stare up at us as they passed by under the plateau. Their eyesight is excellent, and they are quick to detect any unfamiliar shapes in what is, for them, a very familiar landscape. Startled by our brightly coloured tents, they would gallop by and not slow down until they had reached the end of the valley.

ABOVE *Cameraman John Wilson recalling our solemn assurance that mosquitoes would not be attracted to pale coloured clothing.*

BELOW *John Wilson starting a day's hike, loaded up with long lenses, film, and accessories. Under his left arm, ready for action, is a 16 mm Arriflex camera.*

"Wake up," John whispered in my ear. "The storm's over." It was two o'clock in the morning. The dark clouds had finally slipped away to the south, leaving our valley bathed in a soft golden light. It was the kind of scene photographers dream about. Fresh snow blanketed the slopes, and among the hilltops there was a marvellous play of sunlight and shadow. For an hour or more, we experimented with different lenses, using them to find pictures within pictures. Each lens seemed to reveal a totally different aspect of the mountain range. After three days of storm, this was our reward.

Next morning, the helicopter came roaring up the valley toward camp. The pilot, Dan Riopel, knew we wanted to film aerials of the North Slope, and the weather was perfect — bright sun and almost no wind. We sent John and Ross off in the chopper with instructions to "capture the country," while we settled down to photograph the arctic ground squirrels.

The ground squirrels were engaging little creatures, popping up out of their burrows when we least expected it and surprising us with their high-pitched whistles and loud, chattering calls. The young ones were just a few weeks old. While their parents foraged for roots and berries, they chased back and forth on the sunny slope, waylaying and pouncing on one another in mock ambush. When we approached too closely, they would spring apart, dash off in separate directions, and then whistle sharply at us from a safe distance.

Arctic ground squirrels live in a harsh environment. They are at the very bottom of the food chain, which means that almost everything else eats them — foxes, wolves, hawks, gyrfalcons, owls, and grizzly bears. The grizzlies spend considerable time and energy digging them out of their burrows, particularly in spring and late fall when fresh vegetation is scarce. Although the squirrels are not large — no more than a quick mouthful for a hungry grizzly — there are a lot of them, and perhaps the amount of energy a bear spends digging them out is more than made up for by the sheer quantity of squirrels consumed. A friend of ours once estimated the number of ground squirrels in the Yukon in "tonnes per acre"!

In addition to their many predators, ground squirrels have had to adapt to the ever-present permafrost, a layer of permanently frozen ground, which lies just under the surface and has the consistency of poured concrete. The squirrels must choose their denning sites very carefully, because they spend up to seven months of the year in hibernation. They look for dry, well-drained gravel ridges or steep slopes where they can dig down far enough to escape winter's cold without running into the permafrost barrier. Judging by the number of old and new burrows dug into the face of our plateau, it had been a good denning site for generations of ground squirrels. We saw one squirrel burrowing vigorously into the tundra on top of the plateau near our tents. The dirt flew, and by the time the squirrel emerged, its face covered in damp earth, all it had managed to do was to excavate a long tunnel which ran horizontally under the surface.

We were still on our hands and knees, elbowing our way up to the ground squirrels, when we heard the distant whine of the Jet Ranger returning. As it buzzed up over the plateau, the squirrels whistled loudly and vanished down their burrows. Waiting for the helicopter to wind down, we wondered how the filming had gone. I could see John Wilson in the back seat, and from the way he was grinning ear to ear, I had a feeling he had shot something more than just aerials. Sure enough, when the engine finally stopped, he leapt out, danced a little jig, and whooped with joy. "You're never going to believe this," he called out to us.

Soon after they had left camp that morning, they spotted a grizzly sleeping at the bottom of a steep gully. Trying not to frighten it, Dan quickly swung the chopper away, flew on over the next hilltop, and landed. The three of them then gathered up the film gear and hiked back. From a high ridge, they looked down into the ravine and saw not one but three grizzly bears, all wide awake.

In seconds, John set up the heavy tripod, whipped on a fifteen-power lens, and began filming. Ross took charge of the high-powered rifle, while Dan snapped still pictures. The bears lazily stretched and looked up. They could see the three figures on the ridge above, but the bears were upwind and could not catch their scent. Through his long lens, which brought the grizzlies so close that he could see individual muscles rippling on their shoulders, John watched and filmed as, one by one, the bears slowly got to their feet and began to amble up the draw toward the camera. They were curious and coming up for a closer look. But all Ross and Dan could see were three very large wild grizzlies moving deliberately toward them. Hurried whispers were exchanged, and Ross slipped a 30.06 shell into the rifle chamber.

It was not a good situation. The bears did not appear threatening. Nevertheless, they were well within charging distance and closing steadily. John was now getting tight, full-frame shots of teeth, eyes, and immense feet. Never dreaming the grizzlies would venture so close, he was trapped with a lens that was too long. A zoom lens would have given him a wider view, but he did not want to risk missing the action by taking time to change lenses. So he just kept filming, feeling far more excited than nervous. Besides,

as he told us later, he always feels safe standing behind his tripod.

Ross aimed the rifle high in the air and fired a warning shot, hoping to turn the grizzlies away. Nothing happened. The bears gave no sign of having heard it. He fired a second warning shot, this time into an old snowdrift almost in front of the lead grizzly. The shell kicked snow into the bear's muzzle. Still no effect. Nervously, and perhaps too quickly this time, Ross tried to lever a third shell into the chamber, but the brass casing jammed. The gun was suddenly useless. In desperation, Dan and Ross began to yell, but the bears gave every indication of being deaf — or very determined. They approached to within twenty metres and then began to walk, unhurriedly, in a wide arc around the camera crew. As they circled, the bears caught the unfamiliar human scent and, in Ross's words, "left the country," bounding up and over the ridge. John Wilson kept filming until the last one had disappeared over the top.

It was an exciting tale. After Ross and John had finished telling it, they asked about our day, and I was hard pressed to think up something equally exciting about our ground squirrels! Much later, over coffee, we talked about that jammed rifle. Where would Ross's third shot have gone? He was honestly not sure, and we were glad that he had not had to make a decision. It was clear, in retrospect, that the bears had only wanted to identify the strange shapes on the ridge. To do that, they had had to come close enough to catch a scent. Other travellers, in a similar situation, might well have been shooting to kill when there was no need, at least not in this instance.

It is not always easy to interpret grizzly behaviour, particularly in sudden face-to-face encounters, when your heart tends to beat faster than your head can think. John Russell had given us one short lesson on grizzly behaviour while we were at Komakuk Beach. It was advice from a good source — John's father is Andy Russell, the well-known wilderness writer and grizzly expert. "If you come across a grizzly unexpectedly, perhaps approaching you on the same trail, and if he turns sideways and seems to be gazing off into the hills — remember this. He's not admiring the view, he's talking to you. If you don't get out of there in twenty seconds, he's going to charge! But don't run. Back off at an angle so the bear can see clearly that you are leaving." It takes time and experience to learn the correct grizzly bear body language — and sometimes a great deal of courage too.

In the weeks that followed, we explored adjacent valleys and spent hours sitting on high, wind-swept hills, waiting and watching for caribou. Although the north winds were still cold, we now welcomed them; when warm winds blew from the south, hordes of mosquitoes appeared like magic out of the wet tundra. Tundra is an ideal breeding place for these hungry pests. In spring, the underlying permafrost prevents the melting snow and rain from seeping into the ground. The water collects in every low spot and shallow depression, which under the warm sun soon turn into stagnant pools, excellent nurseries for millions upon millions of mosquitoes. Our headnets and bug jackets gave us some defence, but every time the wind shifted to the south, the clouds of insects could be relied upon to make life thoroughly miserable.

One morning we were all having breakfast in our tents. The cameras with long lenses were sitting on tripods, ready for instant use, and our binoculars lay within easy reach. I was about to fetch more water from the stream when I spied a movement at the far end of the valley. One lone caribou was approaching — not quite the great herd we were anticipating, but perhaps worthy of a shot or two. Earlier, John Wilson had set up his photographic blind on the valley floor. It stood directly in the path of the approaching caribou, and John decided this was a good time to try it out. Scooping up his camera, film, light meter, and a walkie-talkie so that we could communicate, he set off down the slope. Ten minutes later, he was inside the blind, about a kilometre from us, with his long lens poking out through the viewing port. The blind's tan-coloured cotton walls billowed back and forth as he thrashed about inside, getting himself organized in the confined space.

From our perch on the plateau, we kept John advised of the caribou's progress. It was trotting along, still unaware of him. Soon it was too close to the blind for us to risk calling John — the caribou would hear our voices coming over the radio. We could only hope that by now John was filming. As soon as the caribou saw the blind, it threw on all four brakes, one front leg thrust out to the side in the characteristic "ready-for-flight" stance. We could almost hear the caribou's mind working as it stared at the strange rectangular shape looming up out of the flat tundra. For a moment or two, the animal stood motionless, and then it made a quick decision. Shifting suddenly into high gear, it put on a tremendous burst of speed and swept by the blind like an east wind. It was an impressive display. Knowing John's skill with long lenses and fast-moving targets, we knew he must have shot some spectacular footage. Just then, John's voice came crackling over the radio: "O.K., I'm all set. Where's that caribou?"

The days passed quickly, and by early July we began to suspect that the main part of the Porcupine herd had bypassed our valley and followed other trails through the foothills of the North Slope. By now, the cows would have calved and moved on into Alaska. Soon they would be returning to meet up in a great rendezvous with the bulls, which were probably still somewhere north and east of our camp. Many of the bulls follow different routes to the coast and lag far behind the cows, never reaching Alaska but meeting up with the cows on their return. Two days later, our suspicions were confirmed — in a most unusual way.

A loud humming filled the valley. Looking up, we picked out a tiny speck dropping below the clouds. It was a Cessna 180 with John Russell on board. The plane steadily lost altitude and roared by just over our heads. As we ducked, John's bearded face grinned down at us from the window. What on earth were they doing? Surely the pilot was not going to try and land on our plateau. It was flat, but not that flat!

Banking sharply, the Cessna turned and came in for another low pass. With scarcely fifteen metres of altitude, and at full flaps, the small aircraft bore down on our camp. An arm appeared out the passenger window, the hand clutching a white styrofoam coffee cup from which trailed a blue ribbon. We threw ourselves on the ground as the Cessna blasted by right overhead. The coffee cup, weighted with a stone, came down like a tiny missile. Inside was a message: "A large herd of several thousand caribou is moving back out of Alaska. We have counted 80 000 caribou just inside the Yukon border. They will be heading for the Firth River south-east of your camp. Another large herd of bulls is still on the coastal plain. Suggest you move to the Firth River area and wait for the caribou there." These were the words we had been waiting for. We were disappointed to have missed the calving and the main northward migration, but now that the cows and calves were starting their return

journey, we would have a second chance at capturing them on film. And the bulls were still in our area.

By late afternoon, we were packed and ready to travel. When Dan Riopel arrived with the Jet Ranger, he reported seeing caribou not far to the east. Although they were well spread out over the plain, he estimated their number to be between four and five thousand. These were probably the bulls. We would try for them first and then head on to the Firth. As we cleared the hills in the chopper, Dan received a message from the radio operator at Komakuk Beach. The spotter plane had just sighted up to 5000 bulls on the coastal plain ten kilometres east of the radar base. There was no time to lose.

Within the hour, John and I were on the ground at Komakuk, loading our backpacks and getting ready to intercept the caribou on foot. Then we realized we had a major problem. We had come out on the first chopper load, leaving Ross and John to finish breaking camp. In our haste, we had failed to check our film supply before leaving. A desperate search of the packs produced just one-and-a-half rolls of sixteen millimetre film, barely four minutes of film time, and we were about to face an immense herd of caribou! If we waited for the others to arrive, we might risk missing the bulls. There was no choice; we would have to make do with what we had. Quickly, we shouldered our packs and headed out across the open plain from Komakuk toward a distant line of low ridges.

Splashing through shallow bogs, we walked, ran, and stumbled for almost five kilometres across uneven tussock tundra, constantly tripping over the high grassy hummocks, which were perfectly placed to frustrate anyone in a hurry. As we ran, rock ptarmigan flushed at our feet and long-tailed jaegers swooped about when we crossed through their territories. Thousands of mosquitoes made the trek with us, but we just pulled the nets more tightly around our heads and tried to outdistance them. Finally, after an hour that seemed more like an eternity, we reached dry high ground with a good view of the coastal plain to the east. Dumping our gear, we crawled up the nearest ridge and peered over the slight rise. Low storm clouds blended into the browns and greys of the landscape, but nothing moved on the plain. For an hour or two we waited, searching with binoculars and uncomfortably aware of the fact that we had nothing to scare off grizzlies. Both the rifle and the flare gun were back at Komakuk.

I was beginning to think the message from the spotter plane must have been garbled when the horizon began to come to life. A brown stain was spreading slowly across the hills in the far distance. Through the constantly shimmering ground haze, we could see a moving forest of dark antlers. There was little cover, so we crouched low, stayed close together, and tried to change the shape of our silhouette by draping ourselves in mosquito netting. Caribou in groups are less likely to panic than single animals. If the lead animals passed by us and did not show alarm, the rest of the herd would probably follow. We sat very still in our own little cloud of mosquitoes and waited as the huge herd of caribou bulls advanced. It was a dark day with barely enough light for the telephoto lenses and slow-speed film. We began to dream of sunlight, but there was not a break to be seen in the heavy cloud cover.

The herd meandered first one way and then another across a front that was almost two kilometres wide. Before long, the lead bulls were just below the rise, a few hundred metres in front of us. As we came into view, the first ones stopped and stared at us suspiciously. Uncertain, they turned and would have gone back had the bulls following behind not pressed forward, urging them on. The momentary hesitation over, the herd parted around us and flowed by like two broad brown rivers.

It was an amazing experience to sit in the middle of the moving herd, to be surrounded by more caribou than we could possibly count. The animals passed by so closely that we could hear the clicking of the bones in their feet, ringing out like thousands of tiny castanets. It is a sound you can hear only at close range, and we were sorry that our tape recorder was also back with John and Ross.

Soon we had used up our precious minutes of sixteen millimetre film recording the spectacle, planning every shot with care so as not to waste a single frame. Next we turned to our still cameras and, finally, when our film supplies were exhausted, we just sat back and enjoyed the sight. As the herd moved on further up the coast, the bulls were silhouetted briefly against the distant radar base. It was a strange visual blend of modern technology and wild nature.

In the next few days, the herd of bulls would meet with the cows and calves returning from Alaska. Then the whole herd would travel back and spread out among the foothills of the British Mountains, where they would spend the remaining weeks of summer grazing and putting on fat before returning south to the wintering grounds.

Flying out once more from Komakuk Beach, we headed toward the valleys and deep canyons of the Firth River. From the chopper, we had a bird's-eye view of the land and a far better chance of spotting caribou. Helicopters can be marvellous "platforms in the sky" but should be used with caution and restraint. They have a very distinctive sound, a deep rhythmic throbbing that carries a long way. Even heard from a distance, the sound of an approaching helicopter can spread alarm among the caribou. In the Yukon, there are strict regulations governing all small aircraft and helicopters flying near the herds. Low over-flights can all too easily start a stampede, and when there are young calves present, the results can be disastrous. Our purpose was not to film the caribou from the helicopter, but merely to use the chopper as a means of locating the herds. We would fly at a good altitude and keep far enough back so that we would not cause any disturbance.

As we approached the Firth, the green plains became speckled with the pale bodies of thousands of caribou. We searched for a place to land. John spotted a dried-up stream bed that wandered through the plain right into the heart of the herd. It would give us good cover all the way. We backtracked about two kilometres and set down gently on a gravel bar in the middle of the stream bed.

When the chopper's rotors finally wound down and all was quiet, we hiked along the stream bed, picking our way through the rubble left by early spring floods and keeping well hidden under the high banks on both sides. At the edge of the last deep gully, we climbed out and found ourselves looking out over a scene reminiscent of an African plain. On all sides, caribou were quietly grazing. Some were no more than thirty metres away, and they seemed more curious than alarmed by our sudden appearance. Calves suckled, cows grunted softly, and groups of bulls lay resting together like members of an exclusive gentlemen's club.

Many of the cows looked tired and thin as they wandered by us. The long migration had been a difficult time for them. With the endless travelling and the strain of giving birth and nursing, they had had little chance to rest. Now they were grazing peacefully, searching for willow leaves and small shrubs that would help restore their energy. The cool, strong winds sweeping across the plain gave them some relief from mosquitoes. During the mosquito season — a time when the cows, in particular, need every ounce of strength they can find — a caribou can lose as much as a litre of blood a week to the insects. And weak or injured calves can actually be killed by mosquitoes. The virulent hordes have frequently driven entire herds to stampede in a desperate attempt to escape the continual harassment.

John and I filmed unobtrusively for a short while and then quietly withdrew back down the gully. We did not want to frighten or disturb the herd, for the caribou would need all of their strength to cross the Firth River, the next stage of their migratory journey.

The heavily silt-laden waters of the Firth pour out of the British Mountains and flow fast and strong across the Yukon's North Slope. Following the contours of the land as it falls toward the Beaufort Sea, the river cuts through deep canyons with high rock walls. Here the Firth narrows, concentrating its force. The current is powerful, and there are many rapids with few places for the caribou to safely cross over. Yet cross the river they must.

From one high plateau above the Firth, a large group of caribou came surging down toward the rushing water. The lead animals were nervous and hesitant as they reached the river's edge, but pushed on by the others massing behind, they quickly entered the water. At that moment, something frightened them. Turning, they splashed out and raced back up the slope, confusion spreading among them. Finally a cow came forward, stepped into the river again, and was followed by the rest of the herd. The current was strong, and although the animals were powerful swimmers, they were being carried for some distance downstream. The bulls and cows had no trouble crossing, but the calves struggled to stay close behind their mothers, nose to tail. Frequently the cows looked back, as they forged through the current, to make sure their young ones were still there. On reaching the far side, the caribou climbed out, shook themselves like dogs, and with scarcely a pause, ran swiftly up the steep slope to the grassy plateau above. For more than an hour, there was a continuous flow of movement across the Firth.

A few cows came out of the water only to turn and discover that their calves were missing. Anxiously, they ran back and forth on the bank, quickly checking out the lone calves and just as quickly rejecting them if they were not their own. There were calves looking for mothers, too. We were perched partway up the slope when one wet young calf bounded up to us, hoping perhaps that one of us was its mother. There were some happy reunions at the water's edge, but some cows never do find their calves, and eventually, when the migratory urge pulls strongly, they will give up and follow the herd.

Further upriver, there was a narrow section of the Firth where the current was even stronger. Many of the calves were being swept away in the rapids, and even the cows were crossing with great difficulty. Most of the herd was already across, but one very small calf hung back, bleating plaintively. He must have been a late birth. His mother had struggled across and was calling to him from the far side, her low grunts just carrying above the roar of the rapids. But the calf had neither the courage nor the strength to enter the fast-moving water. Meanwhile, the herd was slowly moving away from the river into the hills, and

This calf came running up to us looking for its mother. It had become separated from her during their crossing of the Firth.

the cow was torn between staying near her calf or going with the herd. Back and forth she trotted on the opposite bank, calling continuously. After a while, when the calf refused to cross, she turned and followed the herd.

From a cliff high above the Firth, we watched the drama unfold. Without his mother, the young calf had little chance for survival — the first passing grizzly would take him easily. Each summer, large numbers of calves are lost during the migration. Many drown, but others fall prey to predators, particularly if they are weak, injured, or very young. The sudden storms that sweep the calving grounds in spring also take a high toll. Although death is as much a part of the caribou's annual cycle as life, it was sad to see this little caribou so lost and defenceless on the shore below.

Six hours later, the last of the stragglers had crossed, but the calf was still on the bank, curled up asleep at the water's edge, his small golden shape clearly visible among the round grey rocks. He was completely alone now, trapped by the swift river. His situation seemed hopeless. And then, suddenly, I had a wild idea. We could fly the calf across the Firth by helicopter, locate the herd, and release him with the hope that his mother might eventually find him.

The more we talked about the idea, the more it began to make sense. At least this way the calf would have a chance to survive. It would be a huge gamble; we did not even know where the herd was by now. Nor did we stop to consider the legality of our plan. (There are regulations against caribou riding in helicopters!) All of our instincts and emotions told us to help the tiny calf and, fortunately, Dan Riopel agreed to our scheme without hesitation. The calf had just been given a ticket to the other side of the river!

In no time, we worked out the details. While Dan started up the helicopter, we climbed down the bank to get the calf, which was still sleeping soundly. The roar of the river rushing by drowned out the sound of our approach. Creeping forward, John placed his hands firmly around the calf's body and lifted him up. He was surprisingly heavy and still half asleep, but once in John's arms he came fully awake. Two hind legs shot out with tremendous strength and kicked wildly in all directions. John hung on tightly as the calf bucked back and forth in his arms, while John Wilson, carefully avoiding the flying hooves, filmed the first stage of the rescue.

We hurried back up the cliff, John slipping and sliding on the loose gravel and trying not to let go of the struggling calf. It was beginning to seem more like an abduction than a rescue. The helicopter was ready for take-off, but getting the calf on board presented a few problems. I climbed into the back seat first and held the door open while John backed in, trying to control the calf's flailing legs in the confined space — the very expensive confined space! Dan looked over his shoulder nervously just as the tiny hooves narrowly missed the rear window. John, however, was enjoying himself, no doubt reliving his early years of handling small calves on the family farm. Soon we were all safely inside. John Wilson, his camera poised, buckled himself into the front seat, and Ross stayed behind with a radio.

As we lifted off, the calf must have been terrified. I held my hand gently over his ears, trying to muffle the roar of the engine. But once we were in the air, the caribou laid his head across John's arm and settled down, both ears twitching as he listened to all the strange noises. "Just think," said John, "out of 100 000 caribou, this is the only one that has ever had a ride in a Jet Ranger!"

In a matter of seconds, we were across the Firth. Three kilometres ahead was a large group of caribou, with a few single cows straggling far behind. There was a good chance one of them was the mother. Landing well off to one side, we got out and carried the calf toward the caribou. He was no longer struggling and seemed perfectly content nestled in John's arms. We set him down in full view of three cows that were now just a few hundred metres away. If one of them was his mother, we hoped she would come forward to claim her offspring. Alternately, there was a chance the calf might see the caribou and run to join them. We stepped back and crossed our fingers.

One of the cows walked toward us. She seemed to be searching, and our hopes rose. We nudged the calf forward a few paces, but the cow veered away and charged off in the opposite direction. The other caribou took no notice of us or the calf. As we stood in a circle, debating what to do next, the tiny calf calmly lay down and curled up at our feet. I reached down and a wet nose nuzzled into my hand. When John began to move away, the calf quickly jumped to his feet and trotted along behind him. Now we did have a problem — and a big one. The calf was beginning to imprint on us.

Being adopted by the small caribou was certainly not part of our grand scheme, but it was a consequence of having interfered too much with the natural order of things. All we could do at this point was to take the calf back as quickly as possible and to leave him exactly where we had found him. As we walked toward the helicopter, with the calf trustingly following along behind, I had a feeling that solution was not going to work either. The calf had clearly elected to stay with us. We were still discussing the problem when my backpack began talking to me. It was Ross's voice coming over the radio. I dug the radio out in time to catch the end of a sentence: ". . . cow here and might be the mother. She's acting strange and coming very close."

Ten minutes later, full of hope, we were back at the Firth. Sure enough, there was a very agitated female caribou on the flat plateau above the river. We landed, and while we waited inside for the noisy turbine to run down, the cow watched us from a distance, without any apparent fear. That in itself seemed unusual behaviour for a wild animal. Our hopes continued to rise. We stepped out, John still carrying our contented little friend. The cow began to come toward us. We released the calf and took a step back. The cow came closer still, and when she was only about twenty metres away, she began to utter soft grunting sounds. The calf could see and hear her, but we were standing right behind him and, for a moment, he seemed half torn. He turned and glanced up at us; however, when she grunted one more time, he quickly trotted out across the tundra toward her. The cow must have caught his familiar scent. Even before he reached her, she turned and began leading him away. At the far edge of the meadow, they stopped and he began to suckle. It was the final proof that she was indeed his mother and that she had accepted him. It was a happy ending — for all of us.

Much later, we learned that when a cow loses her calf, she will hang back at the rear of the herd, searching, and then return to the place where she last saw it. That is what must have happened in this case. The cow came back, swam the river again, perhaps further upstream, and was still looking for her calf when we arrived with him. The image of that tough little caribou, finally reunited with his mother and trotting away so confidently behind her, has become the strongest image of our expedition to the North Slope. And maybe today, somewhere in the north Yukon, there is a big, powerful bull caribou who feels a slight tug at his memory every time he hears a Jet Ranger.

High on a grassy plateau above the Firth River, we took our last look at the caribou as the great herd flowed away across the plains toward the distant mountains. We were nearing the end of our journey, but they were still continuing theirs, a journey they have made across this ancient landscape for thousands upon thousands of years. To walk the windswept tundra slopes of the north Yukon and to witness part of the great caribou migration is to sense the timeless quality of this land and to hope that this original wilderness will remain forever the land of the caribou, unspoiled and unchanged.

CHAPTER THREE

Nahanni

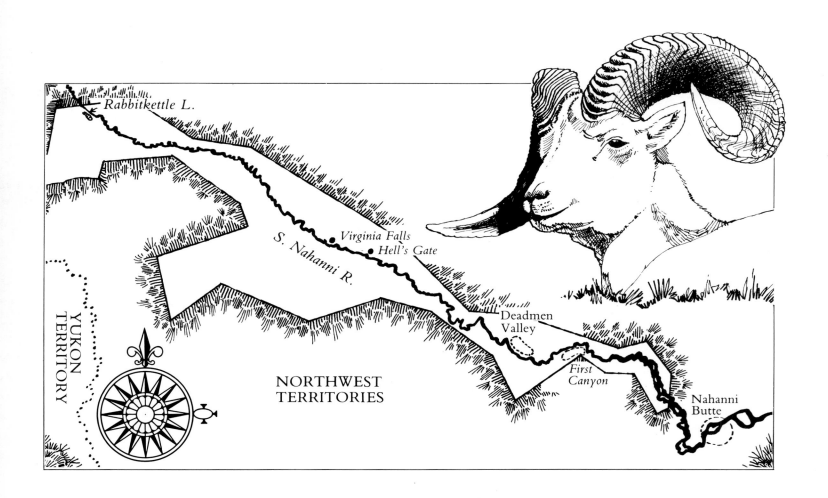

Rabbitkettle L.

S. Nahanni R.

Virginia Falls

Hell's Gate

YUKON
TERRITORY

NORTHWEST
TERRITORIES

Deadmen
Valley

First
Canyon

Nahanni
Butte

THE CANOE WAS SMASHED, its back broken, cedar ribs in splinters, canvas torn beyond repair. Nothing was left of its once pretty design but a memory. It had been much too small and fragile for the river that claimed it. As we fitted the pieces together and tried to imagine the forces that had turned this craft into kindling, we were subdued, for there was tragedy here, and only the canoe knew what had happened.

Janet and I were standing where two powerful rivers, the Flat and the South Nahanni, combine their forces and sweep off in search of the Liard. Art Cochrane, a park warden in Nahanni National Park, had brought us here to show us what a wild river can do to someone who is not properly equipped. "This is all we found," he said, "this and a rifle. We don't know where the body is. We didn't even know he was on the Flat. He must have come into this country somewhere up on the river and hit the Cascade-of-the-Thirteen-Steps. We'll probably never find him." Behind the warden's cabin were two more canoes — both aluminum, both severely bent. Coming down the Flat, their owners had lost an argument with several boulders in one of the rapids. They had survived, but their canoes had been turned into scrap.

As we contemplated the wreckage at our feet, all of the tall tales we had heard about the Nahanni seemed quite believable. Was the man whose body lay perhaps forever concealed by the swift, silty waters of the Flat looking for the gold that was said to be somewhere up the river? If so, he was in good company, a member of a select band of adventurers who have been searching and dying for that gold since the first rumour of it came whispering out of the mountains and river canyons before the turn of the century. In his splendid book, *The Dangerous River*, R.M. Patterson described the 1904 search for the Flat River gold by the famous McLeod brothers. Paddling upriver, they had also arrived at the Cascade-of-the-Thirteen-Steps: "They started off light-heartedly enough and tried to run the Canyon, as dirty a piece of water as you could wish to see, but at the first of the thirteen drops they swamped and lost everything, including the bottle of gold — salvaging only a rifle and thirty shells." The three McLeods survived their trip and returned home, but a year later, the promise of gold lured two of them back, this time forever. Their bones were discovered in 1908 beside their camp on the Prairie Creek delta. One report said that they had been murdered, shot in their sleeping-bags, and that their partner, an unnamed engineer, had disappeared with the gold. But what really started this story on its journey into legend was the gruesome revelation that their heads were missing. Another account said the McLeods had been

Wayne Myers (centre) has just landed his Gazelle helicopter on a mountain ledge in the Ragged Range. Two park wardens guided him in and piled rocks on the skids to hold the chopper down in the event of wind gusts.

found tied to trees, again with their heads missing. As the years passed, the stories picked up more and more colour, leading Patterson to suggest that they were "the gorgeous inventions of the outgoing prospector or trapper, inspired by Bacchus to a bewildering flood of travellers' tales."

Today, canoeists riding the Nahanni current past Prairie Creek can look north into the mountains named for the McLeod brothers — the Headless Range. The valley they are passing through is Deadmen Valley, named not for the McLeods, but for another man who was found dead there. Shortly before he died, as a courtesy and a warning to the next man, he had put a sign on his cabin door: Dead Man Inside.

Another legend for Nahanni. Another story of a missing explorer. The names on the maps of this country stand out like a list of disasters and must surely make people think twice about setting foot in the region: Broken Skull River, Hell Roaring Creek, the Funeral Range, the Devil's Kitchen, Hell's Gate. Did the early trappers and prospectors have a wicked sense of humour and pick the most terrifying names they could, or were they just plain scared of this remote country? Whatever the reasons, some of the names they chose are now found within Nahanni National Park, a place of wild and beautiful extremes, which has changed very little since the days when it was thought to be protected by the Wild Mountain Men.

To some degree, the Nahanni wilderness has been safeguarded by its legends for many years. The name *Nahanni* means "people-over-there-far-away." Somehow the Nahanni Indians acquired a reputation for fierceness; Patterson was told they made "short work of any man, white or Indian, who ventured into their country." This was disputed by a former Indian agent, but it is hard to keep a good legend down, and the stories of the Wild Mountain Men persisted. Before Patterson went up the Nahanni, in the summer of 1927, old-timers at the trading posts tried their best to frighten him to death with stories of ferocious Indians, suicidal stretches of fast water, and vanishing prospectors. At the end of a long drinking session, he realized that "they were saying good-bye to me for ever." He went anyway, and wrote the first clear description of this country.

In later years, dreams of mining gold and other minerals, and the tantalizing idea of all that water sweeping over Virginia Falls, might well have spelled ruin for the Nahanni and its awesome canyons. Hydroelectric engineers, like beavers, are drawn to the sound of falling water. Various plans for the damming of the Nahanni were discussed, but the river was too far away from existing markets, and there was no

While practising for the Nahanni trip on the Madawaska River, we run part of a rapid sideways — not recommended!

convincing market for the power in such a remote region. For anyone who has stood at the rim of Virginia Falls, marvelling at the power and thunder of the river as it splits around a giant column of ancient limestone before storming off into the canyon below, the silencing of these falls would have been a tragedy. Luckily, park planners and many others won the argument in favour of protection and were able to preserve one of the few unharnessed wild rivers in North America.

The river begins innocently enough in a calm and peaceful place known as the Moose Ponds. Serious white water canoeists like to begin their journeys here. Although the true source of any river may be snow-flakes high on a mountain peak, these marshy ponds are generally accepted as the beginnings of the Nahanni. Above stands Mount Wilson, invisibly split by the dividing line between the Northwest Territories and the Yukon. Off to the south-east from the ponds flows a little stream whose clear waters give no hint of the heavy loads of silt the river must bear when its icy tributaries come racing out of the mountains to join it on its journey to the Liard. A few kilometres below the Moose Ponds, the South Nahanni begins to tumble happily along a boulder-strewn bed fringed with clean gravel bars and overhanging spruce trees. For this part of its journey, it is a classic northern river, winding through a wide mountain valley. And for those canoeists who like their water fast and lumpy, the fun begins here, along a stretch of water that has been described as ninety-six kilometres of the best white water canoeing in Canada. In the language of white water canoeists, this is the Rock Gardens, an almost continuous series of rapids full of round boulders. The nature of a rock garden is constantly changing, because the boulders are shifted by spring and summer floods each year. Many canoeists come to grief here, their swamped canoes held by the river's current against the rocks with a force that is measured in tonnes. Even tough aluminum canoes buckle easily under such pressure and must be pounded out and patched before the paddlers can continue.

Cautious and less experienced canoeists will attempt to portage or line their canoes around some of the worst rapids but are still forced to run many of them. Experts let the river set the pace. Down among the boulders and standing waves they go, with a dazzling display of paddle strokes — draws, prys, sweeps, and braces. Only when the travellers are swimming, or their canoe is wrapped around a rock, does the paddle cease to have a function. Wally Schaber, our Nahanni guide, notes in one of his journals that in the short, calm stretches between rapids there is "just enough time for bailing and congratulations . . . crews that don't react are quickly swamped, and must get out, painter in hand, to try for shore."

Another popular access point, Rabbitkettle Lake, just inside the park's north-west boundary, is about a ten-minute hike from the river. There are no difficult rapids between here and Virginia Falls, at least nothing to compare with the Rock Gardens. The lake sits in a spectacular setting. Clear, green-blue waters reflect the spruce trees and the mountains, and echo to the call of arctic loons. To the west, the granite spires of the Ragged Range stand saw-toothed on the horizon. Down at the end of the lake is a small cabin for park wardens, which has a radio for communicating with their base at Nahanni Butte. For canoeists who prefer not to tackle the rough waters of the Rock Gardens, the lake is a good place to start.

A third access point, requiring special permission for landing an aircraft, is on the wide section of the South Nahanni just above Virginia Falls. Canoeists begin their trip here by portaging down around the falls. For paddlers who need a few days to get the feel of the river, this choice may be risky. The first piece of water they will encounter, just minutes after shoving off, is several kilometres of big standing waves in the gorge below Virginia Falls. Many a canoe has overturned there. Starting at Rabbitkettle Lake, on the other hand, gives travellers about 118 kilometres of relatively untroubled river to drift on, with plenty of opportunity to hike, camp, and take side-trips before reaching Virginia Falls and tackling its turbulent gorge (sometimes called Fourth Canyon).

Canoeing on the Nahanni is said to be enormous fun for anyone who enjoys the thrill of split-second decisions among cross-currents, chutes, and standing waves, but it was to give us sober second thoughts as we planned a filming trip with a canoe full of precious camera gear. The only trail through the country is the swift, cold, unforgiving river. One disaster in a stretch of white water would quickly end the filming and cause a certain amount of excitement among the companies that had insured our producers' equipment. Somehow we had to capture several hundred kilometres of scenery and adventure along the South Nahanni and come out of there, in one piece, with enough film for an entertaining hour of television.

Louise Gaulin and Wally Schaber in the Rock Gardens on the upper section of the Nahanni.

As we sat down with our researcher, Jim McLean, we pondered the logistical problems facing us. We would have to carry all of our normal camping gear and food, plus a wide array of camera equipment, batteries, film, recorders, tripods, lights, walkie-talkies, spare parts, and a host of vital bits and pieces. Janet and I wanted to spend as much time as possible in a canoe on the river, but we also needed to get away from the South Nahanni to explore and film the mountains of the Ragged Range, the strange karst country, the Sand Blowouts, Rabbitkettle Hotsprings, Tlogotsho Plateau, and the limestone caves of First Canyon. Although the river is the central attraction of Nahanni National Park, it is the sur-

rounding natural features, many of them unique, that gave this park its World Heritage Site designation. Our task, within a period of three weeks, was to try to film every significant feature, using the river as a thread of continuity. And this is where we ran into some luck. Working in the park that summer, on a charter to Parks Canada, was Wayne Myers and his marvellous Gazelle helicopter. Suddenly the park reserve of 4766 square kilometres began to shrink, and the vital question of how to shoot aerials was solved. We would run the stretches of river less likely to destroy us and use the park river boat and helicopter for covering a large number of locations in a short time. Our two cameramen, John Wilson and Bob

Looking west across Rabbitkettle Lake, just before sunset.

The Ragged Range is well worth the hike from the river. These walls of rock are one of the reasons Nahanni National Park was named a World Heritage Site.

OVERLEAF   A gentle paradise only a ten-minute hike from the icy currents of the Nahanni. We camped for a week at Rabbitkettle Lake, using it as a base for filming trips to the mountains and the Rock Gardens.

Bocking, would travel by boat, or by helicopter when available, and we would all take side-trips away from the river to film the less accessible areas. We looked forward to a busy three weeks.

Before leaving for the Nahanni in July, Janet and I also considered our own canoeing experience. We had paddled many a mile together, sometimes on small rivers or sheltered lakes, and often on large, rough, and windy lakes. Yet there is a considerable difference between tackling an exposed lakeshore, no matter how rough, and a fast set of rapids. The lake, although it can be quite dangerous, at least provides the canoeist with a fairly predictable pattern of waves and usually a sheltered place to wait in until the wind drops. Rapids, on the other hand, demand perfect timing, the ability to read the water and to choose a path while moving at full speed, and skill with a large repertoire of paddle strokes. Another great line from R.M. Patterson flickered through my head: "No — we'd better all have another drink and be sensible and forget about the South Nahanni." Clearly we would need a little practice, if only to give ourselves the illusion of confidence. To this end, accompanied by Wally Schaber, we set off on a spring week-end for some white water experiences on Ontario's Madawaska River. After selecting the rapid, Wally set the tone for the day by running it alone and arriving at the last eddy in a dry canoe and without a hair out of place. Such skill takes years to acquire.

Accustomed as we were to lake and stream canoeing, we found the business of charging through rapids to be new and exhilarating, if a little wet. Surprisingly, the canoe stayed more or less upright in spite of the fact that we ran one short section sideways — a technique that is not featured in canoeing manuals. Our brief white water encounter was fun, but it also served as a caution: our white water skills were not up to

ABOVE *The exquisite tufa terraces of Rabbitkettle Hotsprings have been formed by the mineral-laden hot water as it seeps out of the ground. Some of these terraces are only a few centimetres high.*

RIGHT *The extraordinary mound that has been created by the upwelling waters of the hotsprings. The bright area on the left is the active side, where the flow seeps down from the spring in the centre.*

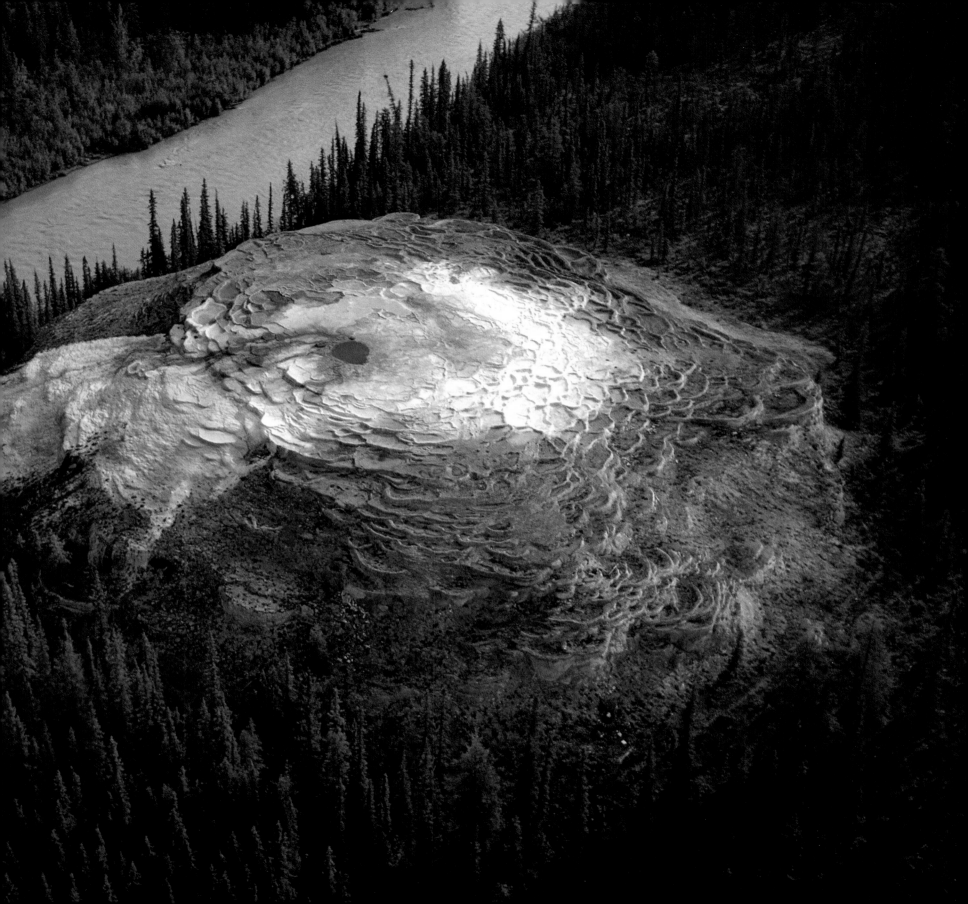

Wally Schaber and Louise Gaulin paddling in heavy rain on the Nahanni between Rabbitkettle Lake and Virginia Falls.

Virginia Falls splits around a giant column of limestone as the river takes its final plunge into the gorge. The air is filled with mist for hundreds of metres downstream.

the standards required for certain stretches of a river whose standing waves, whirlpools, and sunken rocks regularly crumple canoes and frighten all manner of paddlers.

We continued our lesson on our first day in the park. Using Rabbitkettle Lake as a base, we flew off in the Gazelle to the Rock Gardens to rendezvous with Wally Schaber and Louise Gaulin, who had started their trip at the Moose Ponds. Both are superb white water paddlers and a joy to photograph. After filming their flawless performance on the river, it was our turn. A tricky set of rapids, known as Hollywood Chute (also known for a couple of years after our visit as Fosters' Folly), had been selected as an ideal filming location.

After practising separately with Wally to get the feel of the rapids, Janet and I took an empty canoe back upriver. Downstream, two cameras peered expectantly at us, while Wally and Louise waited in a canoe below the last chute to fish us out should we arrive swimming. We put on life-jackets and pushed off, trying to follow the correct line and once again aware of how quickly everything happens in fast water. All went well until we approached the final ledge, where a one-metre drop funnels the water through a narrow passage in the rocks. As we swept toward the drop, it became quite clear that we were not on course for that all-important V of water that spells success. It was also clear that we lacked those finely honed white water instincts that produce an instant correction from bow and stern paddlers. A large, round boulder, well slicked with swift water, smoothly rolled the canoe over as we shot across the ledge. It was the first time we had ever dumped a canoe, anywhere, and we had to do it in front of two movie cameras, one of which was operating at a hundred frames per second to capture the event in slow motion. Sceptics would later accuse us of dumping deliberately "for the camera," but they were crediting us with too much control.

For a week we operated out of our base camp at Rabbitkettle Lake, making side-trips when the Gazelle was available. On one trip, we flew up to the Ragged Range mountains above Glacier Lake. These granite slabs take more than a day to reach on foot from the river, but the trek is well worth the effort. They are characteristic of the most rugged type of alpine mountain topography. The few mountain climbers who have managed to hike into the area and to tackle the slopes have bestowed colourful names on two of their favourites: The Cirque of the Unclimbables and The Wall of Forgetfulness. Mountains are not always easy to climb — or to film. One of the great advantages of shooting from the helicopter was the flexibility it gave us. We were able to circle prominent features, such as a sharp peak, while the mountain range and the rest of the world revolved in the background, giving a tremendous sense of scale and distance. Another favourite technique we used in filming the Ragged Range is called a "breakout." The chopper flies at high speed toward a ridge that is blocking the view ahead, then bursts over it, revealing a dazzling spectacle of valleys and mountains. This is particularly effective if two people are standing on the ridge to give an indication of scale. Janet and I found ourselves perched uncertainly in some terrifying places, while the helicopter made low-level passes over our heads. As always, we wondered what would happen if anything went wrong, and we suddenly found ourselves abandoned at the summit of a hostile and unclimbable pinnacle. We jumped out of the chopper carrying a

The view from the helicopter as we filmed the final drop over the rim of Virginia Falls. You can hike from the portage to those flat rocks on the right.

ABOVE   *Bill Mason is an expert white water canoeist and a well-known wilderness film maker and artist.*

RIGHT   *The terrible turbulence of the Nahanni just before it plunges over Virginia Falls.*

well-stocked pack that included tent and sleeping-bags — just in case.

Finally, we were on the river itself. With great joy, Janet and I stepped into a canoe, pushed off into the main flow, and began to paddle the first of 118 kilometres to Virginia Falls. Nothing compares with that moment of separation from shore, the physical break with the land. Hugging the right bank, Wally, Louise, Janet, and I drifted on the current toward the mouth of Rabbitkettle River, our first stop. Our two cameramen had plenty to do; Bob was off shooting aerials, while John and a park warden set out down-river in a long, flat-bottomed boat. Moving ahead of us, they would stop, set up the camera, and film as we approached, staying in touch with us by walkie-talkie. Our own movie camera, the ever-handy Bolex,

ABOVE   *Bill Mason and his son Paul below the incredible walls of First Canyon, the deepest river canyon in Canada.*

RIGHT   *About eight kilometres of standing waves await canoeists in the gorge below Virginia Falls.*

Delicate and sensuous carvings in soft sandstone have been created by the wind in Nahanni's Sand Blowouts.

rode with us. We passed it back and forth between canoes and filmed one another.

Drifting fast on the powerful currents, we soon arrived at the Rabbitkettle River and beached the canoes. A splendid hike began here, along a trail that took us up the river, across Hole-in-the-Wall Creek, and through the woods to Rabbitkettle Hotsprings. These springs flow slowly from the centre of a huge calcified mound, which stands almost thirty metres above the Rabbitkettle River. The mound itself has been formed from minerals precipitated out of the water over thousands of years. A series of exquisitely designed and fragile terraces radiate out from the springs, capturing the warm water like tiny calcium beaver dams. At the centre of the active pool, the water is a rich dark blue, about fifteen metres deep, with a temperature of approximately twenty-one degrees Celsius. This is one of Nahanni's cooler hotsprings. The source of its heat lies far below the surface. Old volcanic rocks, which are still warm, heat up the rainwater and melted snows that have trickled down from above. When the warm water comes back up to the surface, it is full of carbon dioxide and minerals. It seeps over one side of the dome, its flow slowly radiating over many years, like the hand of a clock, around the mound. Thus, most of the dome is old and grey and weathered, but on the active side, where the water is escaping, there is a glistening of golden film and strange dark shades of red and brown. We explored the mound in stockinged feet, for like a delicate arctic oasis, the tufa terraces are easily damaged by the crunch of too many hiking boots. This is an old and difficult problem for park planners who are trying to protect such features for all time.

Hours later, we were back on the South Nahanni, drifting quietly under a burning hot sun and dreamily watching a parade of majestic scenery slipping by. However, mountainous regions like this one breed their own meso-systems of weather; on the second day we emerged from our tents to see low feathers of mist on the hills and dark, threatening clouds moving in. That day we paddled sixty kilometres in pouring rain, stopping once to pitch a tent for a short while to sit out the worst of it. About three wet hours before we reached Virginia Falls, Wayne Myers's Gazelle came singing upriver. He circled us while John Wilson filmed our misery from the open window. After they had landed on a beach downstream, John set up his camera on a tripod, filming as we approached. We have always made it standard practice to film any hardship caused by bad weather or other conditions as part of the reality of wilderness travel. We beached the canoes for a few minutes and offered some pungent remarks about the weather before inquiring how far it was to the falls and our campsite. "About five minutes," Wayne said. "That is, by helicopter." No doubt he was thinking of the cosy warden's cabin with its woodstove that awaited him. We looked at the map, thought instead of three more hours of cold rain, and then pushed off, our thoughts now as dark as the weather. When we did reach the warden's small cabin, just below Sunblood Mountain, it was wonderful to step inside and brew up some tea before pitching our tents outside in the rain.

There are two ways to approach the portage at Virginia Falls, but only one that a canoeist will survive — keeping to the right and listening for the thunder. Just above the falls, the river is deceptively wide and calm. Then it swings left, and there before the canoeist is about as frightening a piece of water as he or she is ever likely to meet. The Sluice Box, a maelstrom of foaming wet terror, awaits any paddler who has fallen asleep, is unable to read a map, or has chosen the wrong side of the river. Down into this funnel pours the entire South Nahanni, smashing over rock ledges and piling up against the canyon walls as it gathers speed for its great leap over Virginia Falls. In one short, dreadful stretch of water, the river drops over 120 metres into Virginia Gorge, sending spray high into the air, catching the sun, and painting vivid rainbows across the face of the falls in a display at once terrifying, glorious, and free. There is no concrete here, no humming turbines, no men in hard hats making notes on clipboards — just a river that has been left to its own thunder, carving out its own gorge, and occasionally tolerating visitors.

Tucked into the trees at the portage were three canoes and an old Baker tent belonging to a seasoned bunch of voyageurs led by Bill Mason. They were full of stories about disasters in the Rock Gardens. One canoe supported their claims. It resembled a car that has had its bodywork hammered out after an argument with a tree. Bill, who is an artist, writer, and film maker, loves fast-moving water. He cannot look at rapids without mentally running them in a canoe, picking the right line among the rocks, and noting the position of each eddy. Standing at the edge of the falls looking back at the Sluice Box, he thought for a moment and then shouted above the roar, "Piece of cake. Just take her on the left-hand side."

The Nahanni has been chewing away at the limestone here for thousands of years, and Virginia Falls has slowly retreated upstream. Because the early explorers came up the Nahanni, laboriously lining their canoes and boats upstream as they stumbled along the river bank, to downstream travellers the canyons appear to have been numbered backward. Thus, the first canyon today's canoeists encounter is actually known as Fourth Canyon (Virginia Gorge), while the last and most impressive is First Canyon. The gorge below the falls is a winding, vertical-walled valley with few places in the next wild half-hour of paddling and riding the current to escape with any certainty. The moment canoeists push off from shore, they must ferry hard across the current to the far side in order to get into the best position for a long, rough ride through standing waves. To try this run without a well-attached splash cover is to invite disaster, and unless there is about thirty metres of floating nylon rope attached to the stern and coiled in a bag for easy access, the chances of recovering the canoe in the event of a capsize are not good. (This is one reason for travelling in a group of two or three canoes — the swamped canoe can be recovered by someone else.) A group of canoeists who ran this stretch of the river a few years earlier described the experience in their daily journal: "A frightening experience! These waves appear higher than actual when you ride the top, while the trough looks about a mile long as you balance on the brink. There was no way out! Not equipped with splash covers, we simply took more and more water in every trough until we swamped. The canoe stayed upright as we went through. There was no choice but to hang on for dear life and go with the craft."

Once the river has swept out of the gorge, it is joined by several small tributaries. About sixteen kilometres below Virginia Falls, it swings to the right and then sharply to the left, creating an awful turmoil known as Figure-of-Eight Rapids or Hell's Gate. The entire flow of the river smashes into the cliff that is forcing it into a ninety-degree turn, sending water spinning off in two directions. To the right is the Whirlpool, a huge swirling eddy. To the left, where the river is trying to make the turn, strange things

happen. Immense standing waves curl and hiss beside bubbling, upwelling currents and whirlpools. The river is now in torment, blocked by the cliff in front and trying to find an escape route. Suddenly it finds the way, turns, and races below the cliffs. If the paddlers have made all the right moves, they ride the river out of there like thoroughbreds, flashing by the rocks and sometimes smashing through chest-high waves that try to tear the paddles out of their hands. For the prudent, there is a portage around all of this.

Just above Figure-of-Eight Rapids, Wally Schaber issued a challenge to Bill Mason. Would Bill go with him in an empty canoe through the worst path they could find, relying on the Parks Canada jetboat that was with us to rescue them if anything went wrong? Bill quickly agreed. With the boat waiting downstream, and with a well-fitted splash cover over the canoe, they would have an unusual opportunity to try this infamous bend in the river under ideal conditions. They waited upstream while we positioned our cameras. John Wilson crossed to the far side where he could look across into the worst piece of water. Tethering himself to a rope at the foot of a short cliff, he set up a camera with a telephoto lens at water level. The long lens would compress the canoe into the waves, adding drama and providing close-up views of the paddlers. Because we had persuaded Wally and Bill to make the run three times, with the jetboat hauling them back between runs, John could also shoot one sequence in slow motion. Some distance above him, Bob Bocking set up his camera with a zoom lens that would give him the flexibility of shooting a variety of medium and wide angle shots. Finally, Janet and I climbed the nine-metre bank at the head of Hell's Gate and positioned a camera to shoot down into the river to record the start of the run. We had Hell's Gate covered.

One of the most dramatic moments would be the beginning, when the canoe shot out from behind the bank and charged into the waves. Using a radio, we gave John a count-down to roll his camera just before the canoe burst into view. In his book, *Path of the Paddle*, Bill Mason recalled the experience: ". . . Wally took us through the wildest and most difficult route he could find. The waves were by far the biggest I had ever paddled in. As we hit the waves, I braced way out on the right, Wally braced left, and that canoe went through them like a barge." Later he reminded us he would never have tried this without the boat standing by to retrieve them from Nahanni's deadly cold.

Someday the South Nahanni may wear an easier path around Hell's Gate. In fact, there is evidence about 600 metres upstream, where the current has started to eat into the limestone, that this process has begun. Over the centuries, the river has made several short cuts, abandoning old paths in its efforts to straighten out its course. One of the most splendid examples of river erosion stands just over thirty-two kilometres downstream, inside the entrance to Third Canyon. Once again the river makes an abrupt turn, but peaceably this time. Searching for a short cut thousands of years ago, the Nahanni discovered a fault in the limestone cliffs, a crack that could be widened. Slowly, century by century, it forced its way through, eventually opening a channel that today is 91 metres wide and 213 metres deep and known as The Gate. Looming over it stands the graceful, towering Pulpit Rock.

It was while we were standing on the narrow beach above Pulpit Rock preparing to film the canoes pass-ing through the Gate that we realized someone was in trouble upriver. The first indication was the appearance of a strange cylindrical object, spinning in the swift current as it went by. In a flash, Art Cochrane was in the park boat and moving off in pursuit. When he returned, he was holding an orange plastic container. A little prickle of apprehension passed among us as we opened it, for it was quickly obvious that this had been lost from a canoe. Inside were camera lenses, film, and a meticulously detailed notebook and diary. Then another object bobbed into view — a sealed tin containing freeze-dried food, matches, and various essential supplies. As we looked upriver, remembering the fury of Hell's Gate and the great standing waves of Fourth Canyon, Art picked up his radio and sent a call out into the hills, trying to reach Wayne in his Gazelle. If these canoeists were in trouble, they were fortunate to have picked a summer when so much rescue equipment was on hand.

An hour later, Wayne landed his graceful machine like a butterfly on our small stretch of beach. Wally, carrying a coil of rope, climbed into the chopper with Art. Minutes later they were back upstream, circling the Whirlpool at Hell's Gate. Below them a canoe, upside-down and empty, spun slowly in wide circles. A single paddle popped to the surface, but there was no sign of life. The Gazelle moved on up the Nahanni toward Fourth Canyon. More gear was floating in mid-channel, and then they saw movement — a lone, wet figure waving frantically on the shore. Ominously, he was alone. But only on his side of the river. On the other side — cold, wet, and terrified — stood his companion. She was as effectively cut off from him as if they were on two different sides of an ocean. She had no gear — not even a match to light a fire. Neither of them had any food or shelter.

They were lucky to be rescued at all and even luckier that the accident was not worse. Assessing their situation, Wally noted that first of all their canoe was a poor design for the river — too shallow and too narrow at the bow. Secondly, they had no splash cover, and thirdly, they lacked the kind of experience needed for the South Nahanni. "Those are the three big ones," he said. "Any one of them can kill you."

As we left Pulpit Rock and were carried deeper into Third Canyon, we looked up at slopes misting into the sky far above us and began to feel very small. From the depths of Nahanni's great canyons, it was hard to comprehend that once there were no canyons here, just a gentle plain with a young river meandering among the eroded stubs of old mountains. One or two million years ago, when the mountain-building began again and the land slowly folded upward, the river kept on flowing and wearing its way down into its bed. The canyons were being born and would eventually reach a depth that in some places today is greater than the Grand Canyon of Arizona.

Another interesting aspect of this section of the South Nahanni is the lack of glaciation. Like the Yukon's North Slope, this region of the Mackenzie Mountains was spared at least the last advance of the ice and probably the one before that. Thus, the canyons of the Nahanni escaped the crushing destruction of sheets of ice about two kilometres thick. There has been no ice damage here for at least 250 000 years. As we drifted through the canyons, we were looking at a landscape that had been created by the river and its tributaries working unmolested for century after century.

Here in Third Canyon, with Hell's Gate and the standing waves of Fourth Canyon safely behind us,

the river was less hazardous. Not until we reached First Canyon, the deepest and most majestic of them all, would we encounter dangerous rapids. However, we did have to keep a sharp look-out for the little splashes of white up ahead that might signal a standing wave or a ledge that should be avoided. The speed of the current had increased, and hazards like these approached very quickly. In fact, we found ourselves constantly frustrated, because the canoe went too fast for quiet contemplation. We were no sooner upon a spectacular scene, and reaching for a camera, when it was behind us and rapidly receding. This taught us to watch for eddies where we could stop for a while and look around. We encountered another frustration when camped for the night. A quiet evening paddle after supper was impossible — once that canoe is in the water, you are on your way downriver, and the only way back is on foot.

For a few days we camped in Deadmen Valley, between Second and First canyons, sensing the often tragic history of this vast and sombre place. The valley is dominated by the broad alluvial fan of Prairie Creek. This stream flows strongly out of the Mackenzie Mountains to the north, but as it leaves them, it begins to slow down, dividing itself into channels, and depositing its cargo of stone. The creek has been depositing its gravel here for centuries, slowly building up a fan-shaped plain and literally pushing the South Nahanni River away from the mountains. It is an attractive place, inviting canoeists to make camp and explore, to walk upstream, to search for animal tracks at the edge of the channels, and perhaps to try for fish in some of the deeper pools closer to the mountains. But it also confounds the unwary explorer with a confusing maze of wandering rivulets that must be

Wally Schaber and Bill Mason in the middle of Hell's Gate.

Wally Schaber and Louise Gaulin tackling George's Riffle at the head of First Canyon. Louise is holding her brace well, but the river is soon far beyond her reach as the canoe rears up and then rolls over.

crossed, assuring soggy boots during periods of high water.

Looking south from the Prairie Creek delta across the Nahanni and up to the horizon, we saw a landscape dominated by a high plateau. This was the Tlogotsho Plateau, an immense mass of sandstones, bare of trees, stiff with permafrost, and home to the largest herds of Dall's sheep in the region. These slopes are particularly important for them in the winter when the subarctic winds sweep their pastures clear of snow and expose the plants they must have for survival.

As we looked down on the winding glitter of the Nahanni from the heights of Tlogotsho, we could imagine the forces that had created this enormous valley. Actually, it is easy to get the impression that the valley was gouged out by an abrasive river, but this is not quite true. In fact, the land has been rising and rebounding at roughly the same rate as the river has been digging into it. The actual elevation of the river above sea level has changed very little. "Like butter rising up against the knife which is cutting it" is how Derek Ford of McMaster University describes the process. He says that the knife has also been "wriggling a little," an apt description that will be appreciated by anyone who has swept around some of those wriggles in a canoe.

The river at Deadmen Valley is wide and slick and strong as it moves into the entrance to First Canyon. A wicked set of rapids, which can be avoided by paddling close to the left shore, guards the entrance to this last canyon. It is named, with some understatement, George's Riffle, and is also known as Cache Rapids. Once again we set up cameras and the jetboat stood by as Wally and Louise prepared themselves for this stretch of river. Enormous standing waves are the main feature of George's Riffle, and Wally took dead aim. This time the river would win. Their canoe descended into a trough and then reared thirty degrees into the air on the back of a great wave. Wally was almost out of sight in the stern, with just his head showing above foaming water. Meanwhile, Louise bravely but vainly braced her paddle against empty space. She was completely out of the water, holding her brace to the end as the wave slowly rolled the canoe on its side. For a long and frightening moment, Louise was underwater, tangled in the skirt of the splash cover. Finally she came free and reached up for the gunwale of the swamped canoe, which was moving swiftly downstream. Both stayed on the upstream side of the canoe to avoid being crushed against a sunken rock as they were swept downriver — an important rule in fast water. As mentioned earlier, a canoe full of water and driven by a powerful current exerts a pressure that is literally measured in tonnes when pinned against a rock.

The trouble Louise had with the splash cover is one that has worried white water canoeists before. Our own splash cover has no sleeve or skirt around the paddler — just an opening with a stiff rim around it. But it is designed for lakes, not big rapids. Splash covers do not make the paddler invincible, nor should they serve as a temptation to take risks. They keep out a lot of water and prevent unnecessary swamping, but they can be dangerous in a capsize.

Perhaps the most extraordinary feature of First Canyon, apart from the immensity of the canyon itself, are the caves high in the limestone rock. Six hundred and seventy metres above the river is the entrance to a unique and exciting subterranean world — over a kilometre of wandering limestone caves. Dozens more caves pockmark the great cliffs, but many have entrances that are blocked by ice and debris. The most famous cave — and the one that we would explore — is the Valerie Cave. At last, after almost three weeks of carrying battery belts and large lights from location to location, we were going into the darkness and stepping back in time.

Not long after Valerie Cave was discovered, an iron grille was padlocked across the entrance so that access to the cave could be controlled and supervised. This may sound strange; however, even in such a remote place, caves, like shipwrecks, tend to be plundered for their contents. Stalactites are snapped off, fossils disappear, and human or animal relics may be disturbed or removed.

Accompanied once again by park warden Art Cochrane, we stuffed our gear into the Gazelle and climbed aboard. As the Gazelle built up its revolutions with thumping sweeps of its huge, three-bladed rotors, Wayne reached for his headset, glanced around to make sure we were all wearing ours, and pressed the transmitter. "Everybody all set? Seat belts done up? O.K. Let's hit the sky!" Delicately he raised his sleek machine into the air. After hovering and feeling its responses for a moment, he tipped it slightly forward and zoomed down over the river bank and George's Riffle (the only way to run rapids!) before beginning his climb to the top.

As we cleared the rim of First Canyon, we looked ahead to a patch of ground that has been described as one of the most remarkable limestone landscapes anywhere in the world. Geologists call this karst country.

It consists of a belt of land more than forty-eight kilometres long and eleven kilometres wide extending north from First Canyon. Cracked open by the uplift of the land, and then dissolved and molded by many thousands of years of rain and melting snow, the limestone here is an almost impassable labyrinth of towers, deep holes and fissures, cliffs, caves, and rock corridors. Spruce trees and low vegetation hide some of the pitted contours so that in places it resembles a moonscape with trees. Some of the vertical holes, known as natural solution shafts or dolines, have ice in the bottom or perishingly cold water. You could step into one of these and disappear forever. It is not a place to go walking at night! Moose and other large mammals give the area a wide berth. Long, open corridors of limestone, formed by the collapse of the roofs of large caves, extend up to 5 kilometres in length and reach depths of 106 metres. Here the walking can be quite pleasant, with grass underfoot and sheer walls on both sides. Entire lakes appear suddenly, after days of heavy rain, and then drain away, the water vanishing into underground channels and slowly dissolving the limestone to create caves. The word karst originated in Yugoslavia where there are broadly similar regions. The Nahanni karst is unmatched anywhere in North America for its size, ruggedness, and complexity.

We landed on a flat rock, high on the rim of First Canyon, and climbed down over the edge toward Valerie Cave. Wearing heavy battery belts and carrying powerful 200 watt lights, Coleman lanterns, and ordinary flashlights, we walked through the large entrance of the cave into the damp darkness. Neither Janet nor I are particularly fond of deep caves, but this one was different. Valerie Cave splits into three passages. We explored two of them and found, to our surprise, that most of the time we were walking up-

right and making easy progress. The tremendous, although short-lived, power of the film lights made a great difference, revealing detail and distance in a way that no flashlight could.

There are three distinct micro-climates in the cave. At first, the air was humid and fairly warm, but as we pushed deeper into the cavern, the temperature dropped. As it grew colder, the walls began to sparkle with ice crystals. One incredible passage, sometimes called the Ice Palace, is completely rimmed with dazzling ice crystals, formed when moist air from the cave entrance encounters low temperatures and cold rock. Crystals almost fifty centimetres across have been found in this passage. The last climatic zone, at the deepest end of Valerie Cave, is cold and dry. Here the cave traps the cold air of winter, and because no moisture seeps in from above, the floor is permanently dusty. Lying in the dust, exactly where they fell some 2000 years ago, are the perfectly preserved skeletons of about ninety Dall's sheep. Somehow they stumbled in here through the darkness, perhaps in little groups, perhaps one or two at a time. They may have entered the cave in winter, seeking warmer air and shelter near the entrance, and then blundered on, lost and disoriented. Finally, they would have come to a short, but steep and very slippery ledge of solid ice that leads down into the dry passage. That ledge of ice, fed by moisture dripping from the rock above, is still there. No sheep could climb back up — we had to use ropes. Now they lie entombed forever in the Gallery of the Dead Sheep, perhaps the first real legend of Nahanni.

With the lights waning, we picked our way carefully back toward the entrance. The flow of warm air and the gleam of daylight were welcome after our brief descent into winter in the half-million-year-old passages of Valerie Cave. We stood at the entrance and tried to imagine the icy stream that used to flow through the passages we had left, and then looked down at the Nahanni 670 metres below. Once the river had passed right in front of where we stood.

We were close to the end of First Canyon. From our high perch on the rim, we could follow the meandering pathway of the Nahanni as it left the canyon country and divided itself into the confusing channels of The Splits, a braided section of the river where a canoeist can easily pick the wrong channel. One more sparkling jewel in the park's collection still awaited us — the Sand Blowouts (sometimes called the Devil's Kitchen). For the river traveller, the trail to these marvellous sandstone formations is long, difficult, and protected by millions of mosquitoes.

From the air, the Sand Blowouts stand out like a tiny patch of improbable desert in a rich green forest. One gets the feeling that the wind found a toe-hold high on this hillside and then went to work, blasting away the vegetation and exposing the ancient sandstone. This is not far from the truth, except that the first process of erosion was probably rain-water washing away the vegetation. Strong winds then prevented its return, and the wondrous wind-carved sculptures of the Sand Blowouts were begun. Today, sensuously curved columns of multi-hued sandstone rise from a floor of fine sand. Graceful arches, carved from soft, hollowed-out boulders, suggest the work of a sculptor from some early civilization. And through all the formations the colours flow, in shades of yellow, amber, pink, and mauve. When the sun shines, it is a dazzling place that challenges every skill and every instinct a photographer possesses. Native people say there is danger here — that the floor can collapse and swallow you — and they tell the story of a moose that disappeared as it walked among the formations.

Leaving the Sand Blowouts to the wind, which was already at work brushing away the footprints we had left in the soft sand, we climbed for the last time into the Gazelle and flew back to our camp in Deadmen Valley. Our expedition was coming to an end. During the next two days, we would let the river carry us out to Nahanni Butte, to a rendezvous with the old single-engined Otter that had brought us in. A kaleidoscope of images danced through our heads. From its birth-place below Mount Wilson to the ancient history of its caves, the Nahanni had guided us through its own gallery of rare masterpieces, awed us with its power, spun us a few good yarns, and then delivered us back to the outposts of civilization, while it surged quietly onward to the Liard, the Mackenzie, and finally north to the Arctic Ocean.

Sadly, in December of 1983, Wayne Myers was killed while flying for the Royal Canadian Mounted Police. His helicopter flew into an unmarked logging cable in British Columbia. According to his wishes, and as a mark of his love for this wild land, his ashes were scattered over the mountains and canyons of the South Nahanni country.

In the seventies, the faltering momentum toward establishing new national parks in Canada was suddenly replaced by a great leap forward. Nahanni National Park was part of that leap, one of three superb new national treasures north of the 60th parallel. Nahanni stands unmolested, a jewel among jewels, destined, with proper care, to pass down to future generations with all of its qualities intact. It will always whisper its legends and warnings to the traveller, and the river will always be dangerous, but that is how wilderness must be in such a place.

PADDLING THE NORTH SHORE

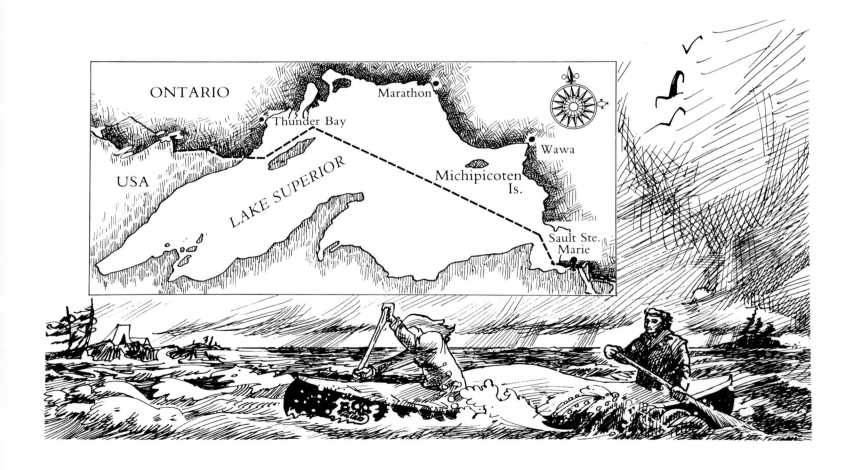

ONE OF THE MOST wildly beautiful and coldly dangerous regions in all of North America is that rim of shoreline along Lake Superior's north-eastern edges where the ancient ramparts of the Pre-cambrian Shield meet the full force of the largest body of fresh water on earth. This is a land that reveals millions of years of creation, back to the beginnings of our planet, a land of granite and quartz and ice cold water. Today, it is a land painted in shades of blue, green, grey, and pink — in colours that change with the weather, the time of day, or perhaps the moods of the spirits who guard it. It is a land of contrast; the breathtakingly clear and frigid water that can render you helpless in minutes may lap upon the fringes of a beach where the sun-warmed sand burns your feet. And, finally, this is sacred ground, the cradle of a people's history and legends and life-style, for long before modern man appeared, the Algonkian Ojibwa Indians and their ancestors were living, hunting, and migrating along this hostile shoreline still freshly crushed and scoured by glaciation.

What must it have been like to live here only a few hundred years after the last great ice sheet withdrew? We may never know. They kept no written history; instead, they told and retold their legends around the winter camp-fire, and left simple yet highly symbolic paintings on vertical walls of granite in a few revered places. To them, Superior was a living force, and all of nature was controlled by spirits of good and evil — spirits that had to be thoroughly understood, re-spected, and frequently feared.

Today's canoeists who pass along these shorelines would do well to heed some of the old legends and stay alert for the rising wind or the sudden squall that may send them scrambling for shore. On one side they face the restless independence of a powerful lake, and on the other, a land of immovable rock. Above them, precipitous overhangs and plunging cliffs guard the land against Superior's power. But in bays and inlets where the lake has slipped past these defenses, a more sheltered world awaits. Here, the lake has spent its energy neatly arranging the rocks into cate-gories by size. Centuries of tumbling and rolling, and constant rearranging by the spring ice, have worn off the hard edges of these once angular boulders; today, many are as round and smooth as eggs. The sorting action of the lake is impressive. Cobble-stones that are small enough to roll under your toes at one end of the beach may increase progressively in size toward the other end, where some are so massive that a pair of black bears could not push them aside. And even as the lake completes this work, the beach may be slowly rising beyond its reach. Thousands of years after the retreat of the Wisconsin Glacier, the land is continuing to rebound at a rate of forty-five centimetres every hundred years. Thus, like finished sculptures being raised onto their mounts, the old cobble beaches have been elevated into neat terraces above the lake, with the highest now standing about 120 metres above the present level of Superior. In some enclosed bays, this tilting action of the land has created a staircase of cobble beaches that takes you further and further back in time as you climb.

It is interesting to stand high on an ancient beach and realize that the lake, which seems so far below, once splashed against the lichen-crusted stones at your feet. Here, too, you may find evidence of human history — curious stone structures, built of beach stones many hundreds of years ago and known today as Pukaskwa Pits. Did young Ojibwa boys, approaching manhood, use these structures as vision pits? Some anthropologists speculate that, for days on end, they would lie in the isolated pits without food, seeking visions and hallucinations that would guide them in their adult years. Certainly Superior's distinctive cobble beaches impart to the traveller a deep sense of human and geological history.

This iron-hard land is not built entirely of rock. The canoeist who slips into a bay or turns toward the shelter of an island to rest and forget the wind for a while will often discover the softest of fine sand beaches, fringed with fireweed and wild roses. These gentle oases may be just wide enough for tent and canoe, or hundreds of metres long, following the graceful curve of a bay. But, although they offer sanctuary and relaxation, getting in and out inevitably involves paddling around exposed headlands — high-risk canoeing and hard work if the wind is waiting.

Sand beaches and blue-green waters generally attract roads and people and all the mechanical clutter and support systems that attend automobiles. Perhaps what has saved a few precious corners of Superior from too much of this is its deadly cold water. Along the north shore it never warms up, and after the middle of August, even the sturdiest boats move cautiously as the fall winds begin to stir. But it was a practical decision by highway planners that really protected about 160 kilometres of one of Canada's finest shorelines. As though hesitant to enter the Precambrian fortress along Superior's north shore, they turned away from the lake up in the north-east corner and very sensibly pushed their road north. This decision, no doubt made for reasons that had nothing to do with wilderness preservation, gave the north shore some breathing space. As Wayland Drew wrote in 1974, referring to the highway planner's fondness for following lakeshores, "anyone who claims the lakeshore has not changed in 200 years has seen the lake from the highway, but not the highway from the lake."

How different the north shore would be if the highway had continued to be blasted through beside the lake, with towns and pulp mills and gas stations and passing lanes where only the winds and mists of Superior now wander. Because much of the shoreline is in fact bordered with high-speed roads, those places that were spared have acquired extraordinary value. These values have to do with mystery and magnificence, or, as described by canoeists Wayland Drew and Bruce Litteljohn, with "the co-existence of power and fragility — of the immensity of the landscape on one hand, and the astonishing resiliency of delicate plant and animal life on the other." Not only does the north shore move travellers to superlatives, but it also confronts them with some hard facts. These are quickly understood by anyone who slips a boat or canoe into Superior for the first time. This is a lake that will not tolerate disrespect and will always test even the best-prepared paddlers. They will soon discover, as the Ojibwa did, that Superior is indeed alive and sleeps with one eye open even on the calmest days. Only the most foolish will ignore the two forces that control this splendid region — wind and water.

Wind and water. Some time ago, we came to the conclusion that nature has a special law for canoeists who are about to tackle large bodies of water with a heavily loaded canoe. This law seems to be selectively applied to weary travellers who are approaching the end of a long trip and are within a day's paddle of a hot bath and real beds. It says, quite simply, "There shall always be a head wind." Frequently, a few hours of steady rain are thrown in, and rain never comes from any direction except dead ahead. Living up to its name and reputation, Lake Superior likes to give you marvellous weather on those days when you are comfortably camped and lazily exploring nearby shorelines and then whip up a ferocious storm on the one morning that you have chosen for breaking camp.

We learned this by experience on a warm summer night late in July, after several idyllic days of hot sand, bare feet, and peaceful drifting among polished waters and pink granite islands. We were packed and ready to go with only the tent and sleeping-bags to roll up before dawn. Always suspicious of the lake, we were constantly waking up during the night, listening for the first hint of a rising wind in the trees, the slap of waves on rock, or the flutter of cotton over our heads. We had planned to steal away at first light, before the lake noticed us, and to be on a new campsite fifteen to twenty kilometres away by lunchtime. But about three o'clock in the morning, the trees above us gave a great sigh, the tent shivered, and a wind began sweeping across Lake Superior from the southwest. Already, it was too late. The great thrust of Pointe La Canadienne stood between us and our next camp, and we were not anxious to try to make it past that ancient barrier in the face of a steadily increasing wind. By daylight, the white-caps were crashing about among the off-shore islands and rolling in to our beach, and we were thankful to be still safe in camp. Superior is just too big, too cold, and too dangerous to tempt with a frail craft of cedar and canvas when the wind is up.

Without question, it is a dangerous place to go paddling, but only if you are careless with planning, badly equipped, or tempted to take chances with the weather. Although the element of danger adds spice to the journey, it is somehow far more satisfying to take on the lake with care and competence. It is also essential to understand how quickly and senselessly a pleasant trip can turn into disaster. Nevertheless, when the wind appeared to be dropping around noon, we were torn between "giving it a try" and staying sensibly where we were. The pulsing energy of the waves was still quite evident but seemed to be weakening under listless gusts of wind. We began to wonder if we could, in fact, sneak away. However, by now familiar with the capricious whims of the lake, we decided on caution, and on observing our rule of making long camp moves only early in the morning, when the winds are usually at rest. Tomorrow at dawn we would try again.

An hour later, across the now gently rolling water, a series of distant rumblings began to murmur a low

OPPOSITE ABOVE   *Our own special bannock recipe has been a marvellous success on our camping trips. This is lunch — soup and a bannock.*

OPPOSITE BELOW   *One day's supply of food for two people travelling light: a cup of oatmeal with raisins and tea (breakfast), a packet of dried soup and a pre-mixed bannock (lunch), and three freeze-dried courses (supper).*

ABOVE   *On some cobble beaches, there may be only a tiny patch of ground flat enough for a tent. When we returned to this beach two years later, the spring ice floes had re-arranged everything, and there was no place to pitch a tent.*

warning in the still and humid air. As a fine haze spread slowly across the sky, the shimmering western horizon turned from blue to black. Soon the wind returned, colder this time. Like an advance scout from the storm, it began to explore our bay, as if to probe the defenses. We drew the canoe high up on the beach, turned it over and stored loose packs underneath, in anticipation of heavy rain. But this storm was gathering itself together and moving very slowly, muttering and grumbling somewhere in the middle of a steadily darkening sky. After making sure that the tent was secure and every scrap of gear was safely stowed away, we set up two tripods on the beach with cameras and wide-angle lenses pointing over the lake, ready for action. And still we waited, as angry feathers of cloud hung above us, twisting and boiling in currents of opposing air masses. In this strange half light and eerie calm, we felt uneasy and vulnerable, touched by some atavistic fear of the unknown. And then a great arch of grey and black cloud reared above Superior's dark swells, captured a weakening sun, and bore down on our camp. Just behind this now classic squall line, a silent curtain of rain swept forward, led by a glittering dance of mauve and purple lightning strikes. Now the thunder was continuous and explosive, and we grew increasingly nervous, crouched over tripods on an exposed beach, feverishly photographing this display of power.

The storm was upon us, and it was magnificent, a wild study in black and white, coloured only by its own brilliant sparks of lightning that struck the open lake half a kilometre from our beach. This was wilderness photography at its best. We kept trying for those elusive pictures of an actual lightning strike, justifying our increasingly dangerous situation by reasoning that the storm was not yet overhead. (This was a foolish decision; the storm was very close and our tripods were natural conductors for the electricity that flies around after a near miss. It is this "step voltage" that accounts for so many deaths and injuries in thunderstorms.) The moment was awesome, frightening, and irresistible — and, most important, we were getting pictures.

Earlier experiences had shown us that lightning is not always hard to photograph, provided we had a clear view of a well-defined storm. Contrary to popular belief, lightning frequently strikes twice or even three times, milliseconds apart, in the same place. This storm was about as clearly defined as a charging grizzly bear, and we hurriedly applied a few tested procedures that usually guarantee successful lightning pictures — accompanied by a good deal of terror. Because the storm was so dark, and the cameras' shutter speeds so slow, we had to use the aluminum tripods or run the risk of having the pictures blurred by the movement of hand-held cameras — to say nothing of the flinching we would add when nature obliged us with a bolt of lightning. Light meters aimed at the grey clouds along the storm's leading edge recommended a shutter speed of a fifteenth of a second, too slow to hand-hold, but slow enough to give us a longer time to capture each flash. Finally, there was the question of when to pull the trigger. Using wide-angle lenses, we kept our eyes to the camera view-finders, staring at the storm, with one finger applying a light pressure on the shutter release. The instant we saw lightning through the lens, we fired the shutter. We often missed the first flash but almost always recorded the second, if there was one. Some lightning strikes seemed to hang in the air for a moment, and these were easier to catch. At home, two weeks later, we counted eleven successful pictures, although a couple were blurred by what was probably a too hasty, stabbing finger on the shutter.

A violent purple flash, much too close, finally sent us running for the tent — as though a few square metres of flimsy cotton and nylon could somehow offer sanctuary! Fortunately, our tent was on low ground among short trees. We lay in it feeling reasonably safe until we looked up and contemplated our nice aluminum tent pole pointing up to the heavens. But the storm was too busy to notice, and soon we fell asleep, lulled by the pleasant drumming of rain on the tent and the cosy warmth of down sleeping-bags. When we awoke, the storm was moving off to the south-east, pounding the cliffs of Michipicoten Island, and leaving behind the angry turbulence of an aroused lake.

That evening, as she read through some historical material that we were carrying, Janet came across this description of Lake Superior written by Reverend George Grant in 1874: "Those who have never seen Superior get an inadequate, even inaccurate idea, by hearing it spoken of as a 'lake'.... Though its waters are fresh and crystal, Superior is a sea. It breeds storms and rain and fogs, like the sea.... It is wild, masterful and dreaded."

This was our second canoe trip along Superior's north shore, and we had corrected the mistakes in planning and equipment made on our first trip two years earlier. Because this is essentially a shoreline journey, without the portages and carrying that is a part of normal canoeing, it is tempting to pack a little less carefully. On our first trip, for example, we took such luxuries as loaves of bread, aluminum camera cases, and just about every photographic gadget we possessed. The result was a badly loaded canoe, with packs sticking up over the gunwales and the hard edges of camera cases and tripods poking into legs and ankles at both ends of the canoe. We were overloaded and vulnerable to breaking waves. And when a swell was running on the lake, which was most of the time, we could land and unload our canoe safely on exposed beaches only by jumping out in one metre of water with one person hanging onto the canoe and the other hauling gear onto the land. Meanwhile, Lake Superior would be doing its best to pick up the canoe, gear and all, and throw it against the beach, which was usually made of stone. After years of rigidly sticking to our tried and true list of food and equipment that would disappear neatly into three packs, we were tackling Superior like a couple of amateurs. Many kilometres of heavy paddling, and the embarrassment of encountering two friends whose canoe was so neatly and economically packed as to appear empty from a distance, further convinced us that next time would be different.

The most important difference about this second trip was that we had fastened a splash cover to the canoe. Our cover is very light, packs into a tiny space, and can be attached easily with velcro and snap fasteners underneath the gunwales. We can do this quickly even in rough water and a rising wind. The splash cover took care of rain problems and allowed us to paddle reasonably safely in rough water. But its real value was in the discipline it imposed on us by the simple fact that now we could not let our gear stick up above the gunwales. Although the cover is elastic enough to allow for some bulging of packs, it must be a tight fit from one side to the other in order to allow water to run off. Before this second trip, we packed and re-packed, and loaded and unloaded the canoe in the hayfield behind our cabin, until the newly

*A classic squall line moves across Lake Superior. Just behind
the lightning is a curtain of heavy rain.*

acquired splash cover would snap into place over the filled packs. Gone were the aluminum camera cases and loaves of bread. External pack frames, which are nothing but a nuisance in a canoe, came off the packs and went back to the basement. Spare clothing was reduced, lighter sleeping-bags chosen, luxuries confiscated from the food supply. Canned foods or liquids of any sort stayed at home. The food box was a desert, full of envelopes and plastic bags containing stuff that looked like sawdust, and occasionally tasted like it. But everything, including the spare paddle, disappeared under the red splash cover.

Although Superior is sometimes "wild, masterful, and dreaded," there was no evidence of this at sunset. The cold front had passed through, and the storm was now only a memory recorded in the swells that broke gently on rocky headlands and tugged softly at our beach. Our world was clean and cool and quiet, lightly scented with woodsmoke and the fresh smell of wet earth carried by evening mist from the forest. Across the western sky, the vivid colours of afterglow hinted of fall; rich tones of red, orange, green, and deep blue fading into the indigo of night, the classic shades of an evening sky in the northern hemisphere. From our own little circle of light beside a driftwood fire, we again felt the sensation of peaceful isolation in an ageless land. Its rugged contours seemed to draw in around us as night settled over the lake.

The dew would be heavy by morning, so we stowed away the gear under a nylon tarp and flipped over the canoe before heading for the tent. Then, for the first time, we noticed an old log that had been freshly rolled over. "There's a bear about," I said, "I hope he doesn't visit us in the night." A half-hour later, we were drowsily reading by flash-light in our sleeping-bags. Janet was deep in a very good mystery novel, a tale of suspense and intrigue greatly enhanced by the dark silence of the forest behind us. Tension in the plot was building — a murder was about to be committed — and she was straining to read the lines in the weakening light of a dying flash-light when there was a heavy footstep on the shingle beach outside. Thinking at once of bears, I leaped out of my sleeping-bag, yelled, and dived for the tent door all in one movement, to find myself staring at a magnificent and extremely upset bull caribou about six metres away. "Quick, it's a caribou," I whispered. "Come and see!" But Janet was busy recovering. Her eyes were shut and her heart was pounding like the hoof-beats of our departing visitor. The spell of impending murder had been suddenly broken by a footstep in the dark and my loud yell. No film maker could have planned the scene better. And so, having thoroughly scared an innocent caribou and startled my wife speechless, I went back to my book.

We were lucky and saw the caribou the next day. After swimming in the frigid water across to an island, he stood for twenty minutes in the warming sunlight before trotting away toward the trees, his velvet-covered rack of antlers held high, and his long legs and wide hooves easily traversing the rubble of rock and boulders along the beach. Later we learned that fewer than two dozen of these woodland caribou were known to be still surviving in the area, descendants of the original herds that had disappeared from this part of Ontario around the turn of the century, after being pushed to the edge of oblivion by habitat destruction and guns. Although a few more survive on the Slate Islands west of here, the future is uncertain for these ancient wanderers of Superior's shoreline.

A rare calm day on Lake Superior.

This stream tumbles into a hidden lagoon, about half-an-hour's paddle up one of the rivers along the north shore.

A favourite bay, where veins of quartzite flow in a mosaic of colour which can be seen best when the water is calm. In the background is a raised cobble beach.

ABOVE *Deep inside some of Lake Superior's bays, these unexpected soft sand beaches offer a totally different environment from the world of rock and rough water along the outer shore.*

LEFT *Every evening we paddled along the shore to find a perfect place to watch the sun go down.*

ABOVE *We took this picture by using the camera's self-timer and experimenting with flash fill.*

BELOW *Early morning at Cascade Falls. The tent has been rigged with its nylon fly-sheet because of heavy rain in the night.*

Next morning, in the darkness before dawn, we broke camp, fueled by porridge and tea quickly brewed up on a small emergency stove. The air was warm and still, perfect for the legions of mosquitoes that had withheld their attention until we were busy rolling up sleeping-bags and tent with no hands free to slap. They accelerated our departure; sunrise found us three kilometres away, paddling hard for Pointe La Canadienne, trying to beat the wind that would soon awaken the lake and challenge us. Certainly the wind would have no trouble finding us. In the warm light of the early morning sun, we were a colourful target — red splash cover, pale blue canoe, orange life-jackets. Even the cherry paddles seemed to glow with new life in the crystal waters. As we drew in closer to the point, the shadow of our canoe began to climb over gigantic slabs of granite clearly visible beneath us. This was indeed canoe country, just a paddle stroke away from the shoreline's gargantuan jumble of frost-shattered rock — a wilderness edge where the paddler feels a silent, intimate relationship with the land slipping by.

The spruce trees hung in the sky on the lips of vertical cliffs far above, sentinels at the ramparts. A closer look at those sentinels revealed movement in their branches. Wind. And ahead of us the glassy lake was glassy no more as a good south-westerly blow completed its journey across the lake and settled down to its daily task of making waves. The canoe dipped in acknowledgement as I hauled out the map and studied the shore for potential shelter, while Janet held the bow into the stiffening wind and told me to hurry up. Ahead lay an island, about an hour's paddle away, offering perfect shelter from every point of the compass and protecting the entrance of a superb bay lined with sand beaches. We decided to run for it. The other

*The soft colours of fireweed in the early morning light beside
the Imogene River near Pointe La Canadienne.*

These little inlets provide sheltered resting places for weary canoeists when the lake is rough.

option was to get out on the rocks now, while the water was still relatively calm, and spend the day listening to the wind.

For a number of reasons it makes good sense to stay close to shore when paddling Lake Superior. Safety is the most obvious one; if you capsize in water this cold, survival time is measured in minutes. And if you can see trouble coming — as we could now — you will have a better chance of landing, or getting in behind an outcrop of rock. There are long stretches where the shoreline consists of granite walls guarded by a minefield of boulders lurking just below the water's surface. This makes for spectacular paddling on calm days when the canoe slips easily through channels where no power-boat would dare to enter. Along some sections of coast, you can paddle behind the protection of scattered islands and hummocks of bare rock, but, inevitably, the wind will be waiting somewhere ahead.

We had no such protection. We were caught directly off the point. Waves were starting to build, and the situation was changing swiftly. We knew that with a good tailwind Superior could go from zero to full speed in fifteen or twenty minutes. And with this happening now, the rule about staying close to shore changed a little. First, we had to move away to stay out of the turbulence of waves breaking near shore. Having done this, we found ourselves in a strange sea of confused water with waves arriving from the open lake on one side and returning pulses of energy striking us on the other. The waves were literally bouncing off the cliffs and trying to return. The canoe began to pitch erratically, and we were soon forced out even farther from shore where the waves at least had a regular rhythm and could be handled with some predictability. But now we were almost broadside to the

wind. Superior had us neatly outflanked and exposed, with a series of manoeuvres that illustrated how rapidly a quiet early morning journey can go thoroughly wrong.

We discussed the most sensible option: turn around and go back, tuck the canoe into calm water behind the point, and make camp. We do not willingly take risks, and there was no pressure on us to meet any particular deadlines out here. While we tried to make up our minds, somewhat encouraged by the extra safety provided by the splash cover, we realized that we were being offered a second option by our canoe, which was behaving beautifully. Broad in the beam, stable and well loaded, it danced gracefully in the waves. Turning the water aside and rising on the crests, it spoke to us of the craftsman who built it, a man who paddled with Grey Owl along the shores of Lake Temagami back in the 1930s. So we set our course once again for the island ahead and settled down to enjoy the wind and the sun and the thrust of paddles. There is no craft more beautiful and satisfying than the cedar canoe in its natural element. Born of the forest, it returns to the wilderness as naturally as a migrant swan. It is a joy to paddle.

As we drifted in behind the island after an hour of some of the most exhilarating paddling we could remember, the splash cover was barely wet. We dipped our mugs in Lake Superior and drank a toast to Bill Smith, builder of a fine canoe. Born of a Cree mother and a Scottish father in a northern Quebec Inuit settlement, he is a man of the woods who can quote Latin and speak to you in five self-taught languages, while slowly preserving the wooden floor of his workshop with tobacco juice.

Now we had reached the focal point of our journey, an area rich in opportunity for quiet exploration and photography. Superior could storm and blow, but we would be sheltered behind a large island, with plenty of paddling room. Just around the shore to the west we could enter a wide, deep bay with only a short section of rough water to cross en route. To the east, a long stretch of rocky bluffs and cobble beaches, all protected by small islets, led to one of the better places on the lake to watch the sun go down. And we could walk and climb for long distances. The Canadian Shield rolled away behind us to the north. Each high plateau that rose above the forest was thick with blueberries and promised magnificent views of the lake. An old, overgrown trail — marked on our map by a local bush pilot — led to a warm inland lake where we could swim and perhaps see a moose. Even the island in front of us featured spectacular shorelines with re-markable rock formations thickly veined with layers of pure white quartz. Every instinct told us to stay here awhile.

You can miss a lot on a canoe trip if you push on relentlessly every day. That approach may offer phys-ical satisfaction, or a sense of accomplishment in terms of distance covered, but surely it has little to do with the enjoyment of wilderness. There is no time to wit-ness the ebb and flow of natural things around you, no long moments spent with camera and binoculars, no silent observation of a storm building across the hills. For us the essence of a canoe trip is being at peace with ourselves and our surroundings, with plenty of time to explore and no pressure to move on.

With our tent pitched on the grassy edge of a sand and shingle beach, we settled down for a happy week of photography and exploration. Every day, we pad-dled in the early morning mist, hiked over to the inland lake for a swim, picked blueberries for supper, and climbed the hills to watch the sun go down. The trip was certainly unfolding as it should — at a peace-ful and unhurried pace that would still allow time for the eighty-kilometre paddle back to civilization. Our best experience was the warm, still day we spent with cameras recording the crystal clarity of a motionless Superior. This gave us the chance to record the union of land and water along the fringes of the lake, with-out a ripple to break the image. From our gently drifting canoe, we could study the curve of the land from its heights above us to its dim green depths far below. It was almost as if the lake had withdrawn for the day, leaving only the startling wet colours of pink granite and shining quartz just below the surface that were so different from the colours in the dry rocks above. We tried hard to photograph these effects, for it is rare to see the lake still. Armed with wide-angle lens and polarizing filter, Janet climbed out of the canoe onto a solitary rock. From this happy perch, she shot a sequence of photographs as I paddled the canoe on demand into the various parts of the pictures she was creating. Photography like this can be a lot of fun — exciting, in fact, when you find yourself in exactly the right place at the right time.

If beauty has been defined as "that which gives you pleasure" then, in this place, beauty was everywhere and pleasure was constant. Nature photographers, whether they realize it or not, can have considerable influence on how others perceive beauty. By isolating and recording those segments of the landscape that excite them, photographers can give not only pleasure to people who have never noticed such scenes, but also alter their concepts of beauty. A mountain may be beautiful in a conventional sense, but the photog-rapher who shows you new ways to see it, by using a variety of lenses that take your eye to a dozen dif-ferent parts of that mountain, may forever change your way of seeing mountains. One of the joys of nature photography is the opportunity to turn apparently simple objects into things of beauty. In film making, the photographer also has the highly effective technique of movement; the camera, perhaps by a subtle blend of pan and zoom, can carry the viewer's eyes through a scene in a way that says, "Come with me, I have something to show you."

Henry David Thoreau once wrote that "a man has not seen a thing until he has felt it," and he was said to have been scornful of those who saw nothing in nature but a picture. These are fair comments. We go to Lake Superior because we do indeed want to "feel" the land we are photographing. Our compulsion to use cameras and to record pleasurable experiences and phenomena is secondary to the simple joy of being there. To explain why it is important to be there is to find oneself struggling for words that are inadequate to describe deep emotions. Perhaps it is sufficient to say that Superior's indomitable shoreline is as mystically appealing as any wilderness region of Canada, with the ability to instill equal parts of love, fear, and awe in the hearts of paddlers who find themselves entering this elemental place of wind, water, and stone.

On one trip we encountered two friends, Peter Garstang and Lawrie McVicar. As they paddled off into the mist, we used their canoe to illustrate the scale of Superior's granite cliffs.

CHAPTER FIVE

Atlantic Encounters

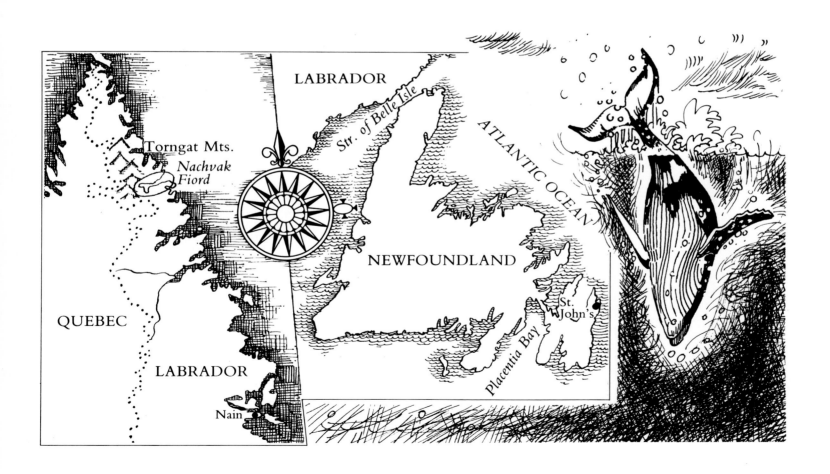

THE AIR WAS FILLED with the tiny cries and plaintive wailings of young harp seal pups. We heard them the moment we opened the helicopter doors and stepped down onto the ice. A few of the mothers had slipped quickly into the sea when we noisily arrived, and now the lusty calls of their abandoned young seemed to be coming from all around us. Two or three pups were lying out in the middle of the flat pan of ice; others were well hidden behind pressure ridges or nestled down between great chunks of blue ice. Some were less than a week old, and in places the ice was still marked with the stains of their birthing.

It was early March, and we were off the northern tip of Newfoundland on the frozen Strait of Belle Isle. The year's controversial seal hunt was due to begin in a few days time. Already the Canadian and Norwegian sealing ships had taken up their positions at the Front, the main birthing area for harp seals in the Atlantic, off Newfoundland's north-east coast. But we had not come to film the seal hunt. In the strait, just north of the island, there was a large herd of seals widely scattered over the ice floes. They were protected from the hunters' ships by the heavy pack ice that had effectively sealed the entrance to the strait. Fisheries officers based in the small coastal fishing village of St. Anthony had located the herd three days

earlier while flying back from the Front, and they estimated the number of seals there at 10 000. We had come to Newfoundland with special permission to film the newborn seal pups, and the weather was perfect for our mission. A high pressure system had moved over eastern Canada bringing clear skies and biting cold. Bundling ourselves into warm parkas, we collected our cameras and plenty of film, scrambled aboard the big, brightly coloured Hughes 500 helicopter, and lifted off from St. Anthony in search of the seal herd.

Flying north over the strait, we shielded our eyes against the glare and searched the icy sea-scape for seals. Below us, the pack ice and jumbled pressure ridges sparkled under the noonday sun. We had good visibility in all directions, but it took time to locate the herd. Each day, the wind and tides were pushing the pack ice further inland toward the Gulf of St. Lawrence, and the seals, carried along on the ice floes, could have drifted a long way since the last sighting. We were a good thirty kilometres off shore, tracing a search pattern that took us first in one direction and then in another, when we spotted the adult seals. There were hundreds of them, well spread out, their dark bodies punctuating the ice like black dashes as they lay beside the narrow leads of open water. We flew on, searching for a landing site, then settled down on the helicopter's fat rubber pontoons, waiting impatiently for the rotors to stop turning and the scream of the engine to die away before stepping out.

We moved quietly through the nursery of ice, always keeping a watchful eye out for the mothers and taking extra care not to step backward into the open air holes. The pups seemed gentle, trusting little creatures. As we knelt beside them, they would stop crying and gaze up at us curiously with dark, luminous eyes, each one complete with a tiny tear-drop. Of all nature's young animals, the harp seal pup must surely be the most beautiful and appealing. They soon proved to be charming subjects for photography. John lay flat on his stomach and one pup wriggled over, shoving a black nose and long, drooping whiskers right up against the camera's super wide-angle lens. And the one that I was trying to film seemed much more interested in being cuddled. It lay back in my arms while I tried to take light readings, its eyes half-closed in a picture of perfect contentment. (Later we learned the pup had probably gone into a trance, a defensive mechanism that harp seals will use if they feel threatened.)

The pups were already fat and healthy looking. Their small, round bodies and bulging stomachs were encased in a warm blanket of white fur, the famous "white coats" they wear for a few weeks after birth until their darker fur grows in. Harp seals are born with almost no fat on their bodies. But they grow quickly, nursing almost constantly on their mothers' milk, a thick creamy substance that is almost twelve times as rich in butterfat as cow's milk. In just two weeks, the pups can triple their birthweight, and by the time they take to the water at the age of four weeks, a thick layer of blubber will have formed under their fur, to give them warmth as well as buoyancy in the cold Atlantic.

As we moved across the colony, the absent mothers began to return, propelling their fat bodies up through the air holes and onto the ice in one great fluid motion. They had no difficulty finding their rightful offspring. Each pup has its own unique scent, and at birth the mother carefully sniffs her newborn all over, imprinting its special smell on her memory. From that moment, she will always find her pup among the many others scattered over the ice floe. A few seconds of mutual sniffing, nose to nose each time she returns, will bring instant recognition. And she will accept no other pup. We watched one hungry youngster slither hopefully up to the wrong mother only to be roughly rebuffed. Another pup spent nearly an hour nestled up to one of the helicopter's rubber pontoons. Perhaps he was finding something very familiar in the big, black shape.

The females were amazingly tolerant of our presence. We moved very slowly among them, giving them plenty of time to become accustomed to us and making no sudden movements that would cause alarm. Usually when we came near, they would leave, slipping away through the nearest air hole or lead. There was only one mother who showed signs of aggressive behaviour. I had set my tripod down too close to her pup, and she came humping across the ice toward me, snorting loudly, her head and neck held high in a threatening posture. I backed off immediately. Each time I tried to move closer, she would come at me again. Finally, I was all set to pack up and walk away when she suddenly seemed to lose interest. Hauling her sleek body over to an open lead, she slid gracefully into the sea, leaving me behind on the ice with her pup. This little one, however, was not nearly so trusting as the others. Its pink mouth opened in a miniature snarl when I bent down, and tiny, sharp teeth tried to bite their way into my mittened hand.

Born into a wilderness world of snow and ice and water, young seal pups must grow very quickly, for their nursery is not safe. Ice is constantly moving, shifting, breaking apart, melting. All too easily, pups can be crushed beneath tumbling pressure ridges or separated from their mothers as the ice floes drift apart. Or they can suddenly find themselves plunged into the icy water before their small bodies are adequately protected against its terrible cold.

By the time these pups were two or three weeks old, their mothers would be abandoning them and taking to the sea in search of mates. The pups would be on their own. They would be fat, and well able to survive without food for another two weeks. Until they learned to swim and feed on shrimp and krill, they would be protected and nourished by the thick layer of blubber that was formed from their mothers' rich milk during their first few weeks of life. It is, as Fred Bruemmer has called it, their "mother's legacy."

Once our filming was completed, we slowly and reluctantly worked our way back across the ice floe to the waiting helicopter, treasuring these final moments among the seals and trying to commit all the many intimate images to memory. At the helicopter, the young pup was still stretched out blissfully beside the big pontoon, his eyes tightly closed. He cried in protest as John gently moved him clear, but we knew his mother would soon find him again once we had left.

As the chopper rose and thundered south toward the mainland, I could see beyond the ice floe to where wide areas of ice were beginning to open up. In the weeks ahead, the seals' icy nursery would gradually disappear as the floe broke apart and melted. The pups would then have to adapt to a new and a watery world. But they would have survived their first few weeks, the most difficult and hazardous period of their lives. With the coming of spring, the young seals would head eastward, swimming out through the Strait of Belle Isle to the open Atlantic to begin a long migratory journey up the coast of Labrador to the Arctic. And at the same time, but far to the south, other migrant travellers would just be arriving — giant mammals of the sea returning once more to Newfoundland from the Caribbean.

"There, over the bow!" John yelled, as a humpback whale suddenly broke the surface of the glassy water in front of the boat. It blew, then rolled forward in a slow shallow dive, giving us a tantalizing glimpse of an immense body as it slid smoothly back beneath the sea. Leaning over the side, our eyes glued to the swirl of bubbles where the whale had disappeared, we heard another one rise and blow from the opposite side of the boat. And then two more appeared. We were surrounded by humpbacks!

For more than an hour, we had been drifting on the calm sea with the fishing boat's engine switched off. Somewhere beneath us in the cold waters of Placentia Bay, we knew there were whales. From a distance, we had heard the loud "whoosh" as they came to the surface to breathe, expelling air and refilling their huge lungs. The sound echoed across the bay, and the exhaled breath rose into the air like fat, misty balloons, marking the whales' location and clearly identifying them, by the shape of their spouts, as humpbacks.

It was early June, and we were once again in Newfoundland, this time off the south coast in some of the richest waters in the world for whale watching. That morning, after waiting more than three hours for the fog to lift, we had steamed out from the harbour at Argentia in a "Cape Islander" fishing boat, whose broad beam and upswept bow were designed to handle the high winds and rough sea on Canada's east coast. The day was heavily overcast, and once the fog had lifted, the wind came up, making it hard to hear the whales blowing in the bay. And it was even more difficult to photograph them. Although we quickly pin-pointed its position every time one blew, by the time our slow-moving vessel had chugged over to the spot, the whale was nowhere to be seen. It was a frustrating exercise. Even when a humpback flung itself completely out of the water in a spectacular breach less than a half kilometre away, sending up a great wall of spray as it crashed back into the sea, we were still too far away for the frame-filling shots we wanted.

Finally, late in the afternoon, the wind dropped and the sea became still. When two more whales blew not far ahead of the boat, we took our chances and cut the engine, waiting and hoping that they would re-appear somewhere close by. Then, after a long hour, it happened. Again and again, the whales came to the surface, filling the air with the sound of their great breaths and churning the water into white froth as they dived. Some of them were close to fifteen metres long and might have weighed up to forty tonnes. There were now seven circling our boat. Three surfaced and swam straight toward us, side by side. As they reached the Cape Islander, two passed in front of our bow and the third dipped down and swam under the boat, rocking it gently. I waited expectantly for the humpback to come up on the other side, but instead it hung motionless beneath us, its shadowy

form nearly dwarfing the Cape Islander. From the port side, long flippers gleamed through the water like fingers of white ice, and from the starboard side, we could see the outline of a huge tail fluke. There were a few moments of high tension on board. What was the whale going to do? I had a vision of the humpback rising suddenly and tossing the Cape Islander from its back like a tiny toy. But fortunately, the giant shadow came up slowly alongside us and blew loudly. A cloud of fishy-smelling, oily mist settled over us like a fine net just as John was opening his camera to change film. We were learning very quickly that the first rule in photographing whales at close range is to keep your equipment well protected!

For the next hour and a half, the humpbacks seemingly played around our drifting boat. Sometimes they would lie on the surface, waving their flippers back and forth in the air, then slapping them against the water with resounding whacks. Or they would spy-hop, lifting their massive heads up out of the water until their eyes were clear of the sea. And sometimes, when they blew close to the boat, we thought that we could hear a different sound, an altered note in their blows as though they were communicating with one another at the surface. It was almost a vocalization, and we began to sense that great intelligence in the waters. Were we watching them or were they watching us ?

Photographing whales can be compared to photographing icebergs, for most of their great mass is hidden underwater. Each time the humpbacks rose to draw breath, breaking the surface like sleek submarines, our still cameras could record only a small portion of their backs as they rolled and dived. Trying to film their behaviour and at the same time capture some sense of their huge size was not easy. Although one whale breached not far from us, we were both caught with wide-angle lenses on our cameras and missed the action. When the whales dived close to the boat, however, in a deep plunge that is called sounding, we had more luck. As the whale rolls forward and begins to dive, its body arches sharply and the broad tail fluke, cascading water from its saw-toothed edge, lifts clear of the sea. This dramatic view of the tail fluke is not difficult to photograph. It is merely a question of anticipating when the whale is going to sound, watching for that arched back, and then pressing the shutter at the best moment. An electric winder comes in handy, because you can record the complete action, frame by frame, without ever having to take your eye away from the view-finder to rewind. I lost a number of good pictures of the humpbacks sounding around the boat by being a little too quick on the trigger — pressing the shutter a fraction of a second too soon and not having time to reshoot before the fluke slipped beneath the sea. Once a humpback has sounded, there is plenty of time to think about the lost shots — the whale has taken enough air to last it up to twenty minutes underwater, and there is no way to tell when or where it will resurface.

The tail fluke is the most distinctive part of the humpback. It carries a unique pattern of black and white markings on the underside that identifies each whale as clearly as a set of finger-prints. By photographing tail flukes, whale researchers can recognize and track whales anywhere on their range. Eighteen hundred individual humpbacks have been identified in the north-east Atlantic region, enabling researchers to learn more about their behaviour patterns and migratory movements.

The humpbacks swam back and forth under the Cape Islander many times, rocking it from side to side with their turbulence. For us it was an incredible experience, but our captain was having second thoughts about all the attention his comparatively small vessel was receiving from these gentle giants. He became even more worried when he opened the wheel-house window and found himself staring into the eye of a humpback that had chosen that precise moment to spy-hop. The window was closed with a slam, and it was amazing how many good reasons the captain could find for returning immediately to safe harbour!

Much later, we learned the meaning of the whales' apparently unusual behaviour as they cavorted about our boat. During breeding, a number of males will compete for the attentions of a single female by showing off. They will swim very close, spy-hop, and slap the water with their flippers in a courtship display meant to impress her. It is possible that these seven whales were responding to our silent, drifting boat in much the same way. We were being courted!

Unable to resist taking advantage of this perfect opportunity to dive with whales, John Wilson donned his wet suit and went over the side. Swimming alone in the cold Atlantic is dangerous. We did not have a second diver standing by, suited up and ready to spring to John's aid if he got into trouble, so we kept him on the end of a leash, a good sixty metres of strong rope that would float. It would limit his range and filming activities somewhat, but there was no telling what might happen once he was among the humpbacks.

John had no trouble finding the whales. One came up beneath him and glided by so closely that he could look into its great eye. Another one swam between him and the boat, passing under his safety line. As the massive shape went by, we called out a warning, but John was too busy filming something ahead of him to worry about what was behind. Getting close enough to the whales was not John's problem; his difficulty was in trying to film them. They were as big as buses, and when they came near, the camera could see only part of the white flippers gleaming eerily through the water, or the hint of a tail fluke fading in and out of the dark depths below. Even the super wide-angle lens could not take them all in. When John backed off, trying for a wider, looser view, the water became too cloudy to see much of anything. He did manage to get a few rather mysterious images of shadowy forms moving about, but for the most part, he was just enjoying the experience of being among the whales and sharing a little of their undersea world.

Whales have been in Newfoundland's coastal waters for millions of years. Their ancestry goes back to the age of the dinosaurs when whales evolved from cloven-hoofed land mammals that, for some unknown reason, chose to return to the sea. For nearly 300 years after the first Europeans arrived on the coast of North America, whales and fishermen shared the ocean's wealth and lived in relative peace with one another. But then, in the 1800s, the Industrial Revolution began, and captains of industry soon learned the value of whale oil to light lamps and fuel machines. The chase was on. Many whale species, the humpbacks among them, were pushed to the threshold of extinction. Today, the humpbacks and most other large whales are protected in Canadian waters, and a new industry, tourism, has replaced whaling. Every spring, an increasing number of eager visitors, heavily laden with cameras and binoculars, brave the cold winds and rough seas to see the whales return and to experience the wonder of whale watching. Of all the large whale species, the humpbacks are the most acrobatic, and it is an unforgettable experience to be among them.

The new interest in whale watching was not the only story that had brought us to Newfoundland. During the mid-1970s, the humpbacks returned each spring from their wintering grounds in the Caribbean as usual, but instead of going to their traditional feeding grounds on the Grand Banks, they came much closer to shore in a new feeding pattern. While this meant good sightings for whale watchers, it had a far greater significance. The humpbacks' favourite food is capelin, a small silvery fish. It was being caught in enormous numbers during these years by large commercial fishing fleets, particularly the Soviet and Norwegian fleets, which were operating in the off-shore waters. Once the full extent of the depletion in capelin stocks became known, the fishing grounds were closed, but by that time the whales had moved to the in-shore waters where large schools could still be found. It was here that the whales came into direct conflict with local fishermen, a conflict that had costly and sometimes tragic results.

Swimming peacefully along the shore in their search for food, the humpbacks accidentally blundered into the underwater fishing gear, notably the large cod traps. Sometimes they managed to break free, towing the fishing gear away with them, but more often they became hopelessly entangled in the strong synthetic ropes and webs. If they were trapped and held near the surface, they were still able to breathe; but if they were caught in deeper water, they soon drowned. Nearly half of all the whales that collided with the cod traps in the late 1970s were found dead. In most cases, it was the immature whales, hunting capelin for the first time, that got into trouble. Older whales soon learned to avoid the traps, particularly if they were set out in the same place each season. Minke, pothead, and finback whales, as well as basking sharks, also collided with the fishing gear. Nevertheless, it was the humpbacks that caused the most serious damage. For the fishermen, the results of whale collisions were measured in thousands of dollars for net repairs and vital time lost during the short fishing season. They were angry and some argued for a return to whaling.

Clearly something had to be done, not only to help the fishermen, but also to rescue the whales. Hoping to find a solution to the growing problem, a small group of researchers came together at Memorial University in St. John's. They formed the Whale Research Group in 1979 under the direction of Dr. Jon Lien. Their aims were twofold: to help free the trapped whales and to try to prevent further collisions.

Knowing that time was of the essence if trapped whales were to be freed alive, group members set up a twenty-four hour telephone "hot line" so that fishermen could report collisions the moment they occurred. As soon as a call came in, a trained crew swung into action, armed with specially designed tools for cutting heavy nets and ropes, and prepared to dive if necessary. Often when they arrived on the scene, the whale was already dead, but at other times their rescue attempts were successful, and they had the satisfaction — and the good feeling — that comes with watching a liberated whale swim away, unharmed.

The whale researchers learned a great deal about releasing trapped whales during their first two seasons. And they had considerable success: of the thirty-one humpbacks entangled in 1981, eight died but twenty-three were freed. But the central problem still remained: how to keep the whales out of the fishermen's nets. Could they be warned away before they blundered into the cod traps? Group members first experimented with underwater alarms that could be attached to the nets. In spite of their efforts, however, the alarms were not a great success and the researchers decided to try another approach. They began to look at the traditional design of cod traps, wondering whether it could be changed or altered in such a way as to make the traps "whale proof."

Fortunately, even while the whale researchers develop new designs for cod traps, the humpback problem is beginning to solve itself. Capelin stocks in the off-shore waters have begun to recover, and the whales are moving back out to their traditional feeding grounds on the Grand Banks. There are fewer whales colliding with fishing gear now, and the damage to nets is only a fraction of what it was during the late 1970s. As Dr. Lien notes, with the researchers helping to free trapped whales and with the establishment of a cod trap depot where fishermen can get immediate replacement for damaged nets, "things are going well and the hard feeling against the humpbacks is disappearing." Even more important, fishermen have been learning to free trapped whales themselves and these close encounters have done much to help change their attitude. A happy ending to this story seems likely, both for the humpbacks and for the fishermen.

Late in the day, the sun finally slipped clear of the heavy cloud cover that had been with us all afternoon. The seven whales still circled our boat, passing back and forth underneath and coming up alongside, their wet forms glistening in the red sunset as they broke the surface. Then just as the sun was sinking below the horizon, they left us. For a moment, the vapour balloons of their final blows hung in the air, back-lit in the soft golden light. Then they too were gone. The Cape Islander coughed and snorted back to life,

BELOW   *A young harp seal pup, full of milk and warmed by the March sun.*

OPPOSITE ABOVE   *A humpback whale beginning a deep dive. The distinctive markings on the tail fluke are like finger-prints, providing researchers with a means of identifying individual whales.*

OPPOSITE BELOW   *The giant fluke of a humpback gleams underwater as the whale rises to the surface and blows.*

breaking the stillness and the magical moment. For us, it had been an amazing experience to be among the whales; perhaps, as John reflected later, the best wildlife experience of our lives.

Deep in a misty fiord on the west coast of Greenland, an iceberg calves from the giant Jakobshavn Glacier. Sixty metres high, the colossal chunk of ice splits free from the toe of the glacier and plunges headlong into the waters of Baffin Bay. As the icy fragment crashes

ABOVE *A telephoto lens isolates designs created by sun and wind and sea on a grounded iceberg.*
OPPOSITE *Photographing icebergs can be tricky. We aimed our spot meters at the light blue tones underwater so that they would not be fooled by the glare.*

into the sea, a curtain of salt spray rises and the waters boil, sending out a tidal wave large enough to swamp a small boat should any dare to come near. Another iceberg is ready to begin its long voyage south.

ABOVE   *One of Labrador's rock walls. A few adventurous mountain climbers travel by small boat along this dangerous shoreline with sheer cliffs on one side and the stormy Atlantic on the other.*

LEFT   *Nearly every bay along the Labrador coast contained an iceberg, part of the silent fleet that drifts down each summer from Greenland.*

The granite rock walls and inland fiords of northern Labrador's coast make it one of the most spectacular shorelines in Canada.

Every day during July and August, the Jakobshavn Glacier releases 20 to 30 million tonnes of its ice to the sea — and it is just one of Greenland's sixteen glaciers that together spawn more than 20 000 icebergs a year. Many of them float silently down Canada's east coast, riding the cold Labrador Current like mountains of polished porcelain. Some drift into bays along the coast and become grounded; others sail on to melt in the warmer waters of the Gulf Stream on Newfoundland's Grand Banks; and still others find their way into the shipping lanes south of the 48th parallel where their position and course will be carefully monitored and broadcast. Some icebergs live only a year or two; others can roam the arctic seas for a decade.

If Newfoundland's waters are among the richest in the world for whale watching, then those of Labrador are, without question, among the richest for iceberg watching. So many of these icy giants come parading down from Greenland each summer that the coastal waters have been aptly nicknamed "Iceberg Alley." In July, we found ourselves once again on board a small fishing vessel, this time heading out to sea from Nain, the northernmost community in Labrador.

East of Nain, beyond the outer islands and up along the coast, we encountered the first of many grounded icebergs. There was no telling how long it had been there, perhaps a year or two, maybe longer. It rose nearly forty-five metres in the air, and the long, smooth furrows worn into its sides were the old water lines showing how it had tilted in the past. Approaching a grounded iceberg in a small boat can be highly dangerous, but we persuaded the captain to take us as close as he dared while we filmed. All too often, towering pinnacles of ice weighing several tonnes can break off without warning and the iceberg can roll over unexpectedly.

There is nothing so awesome or compelling as an iceberg. From the moment it is born, sun and wind and water go to work molding and sculpting, constantly changing its shape and texture. Nine-tenths of an iceberg's great mass is underwater, and as that ice slowly begins to melt, the centre of gravity shifts and the iceberg tilts and turns, finding a new position in the water. And part of the wonder of icebergs is knowing their great age. If you break a small piece off and put it in a glass of water, the water will fizz as the trapped air escapes, air that became locked in the ice when the parent glacier first formed. That ice — and the air — could be many thousands of years old.

Slowly we chugged around the iceberg, using a variety of camera lenses and finding so many different shapes, angles, patterns, and colours that we soon realized one could spend a whole day photographing a single berg. In places, its sides were as smooth and as polished as glass; others were worn and weathered into fascinating shapes and features. Taking a boat trip around a grounded iceberg is a rewarding experience, and one that we highly recommend, but remember the dangers of going too close.

The same Labrador Current that sweeps down the coast bearing gifts of arctic icebergs is also responsible for much of Labrador's climate: the sudden storms, thick fog, chilling winds even in summer, and the long, cold winters. This is a sub-arctic landscape, a harsh and elemental land, the land "God gave to Cain." It is also the most easterly part of the Canadian Shield, whose rocks are billions of years old, scraped, scoured, and worn smooth by glacial action. Only the very tips of the Torngat Mountains, lying four hundred kilometres north of Nain near the top of Canada's eastern mainland, escaped the mantle of ice. Frequently swept by storms or lost in low cloud and

The Torngat Mountains near the top of Labrador are frequently veiled in cloud and mist.

Woodland caribou bulls with the largest set of antlers we had ever seen.

mist, they are sharp and razor-backed. And today they are being discovered by mountain climbers who are drawn to the mountain range by the lure of its un-climbed peaks and the challenge of climbing in such a remote and spectacular place. Everything we had heard about the Torngats aroused our interest, but getting there was not going to be easy. There are no roads leading out of Nain. Any travelling must be done in small boats or on chartered aircraft.

Running deep into the heart of the mountains near the top of Labrador is a superb salt-water fiord called Nachvak. Nearly forty-eight kilometres long, it serves as a highway into the Torngats for anyone brave enough to risk the journey from Nain by small boat up the coastline. Travellers who opt for the coastal route are faced with sheer cliffs on one side, the treacherous

Our campsite at the head of Nachvak Fiord in northern Labrador.

Atlantic on the other, and nothing between but their own courage and sheer determination. Fortunately, at the end of the fiord there are calm waters for small aircraft landing on floats. But whether the journey is made by boat or airplane, the trip is neither easy nor predictable. Northern Labrador is one of the worst areas in Canada for sudden weather changes.

Our goal was to reach the fiord, but a quick survey of the available boats at Nain was discouraging. Nowhere could we find a reliable boat that had a good engine and was large enough to brave the Atlantic waves. The best ones were away with their Inuit owners at arctic char fishing camps. Our growing fears about the long coastal trip were heightened by the faint calls for assistance coming in by radio from a group of climbers stranded about 160 kilometres to the north, with engine failure on two boats.

With good fortune, we were able to split a charter on a Twin Otter with a group of climbers, and our problem of reaching the Torngats was quickly solved — provided the weather co-operated. More days of impatient waiting followed. Either the weather was bad at Nain but good in the north, or sunny in Nain but raining in the Torngats. Finally, a high-pressure ridge moved in and we were on our way.

The Twin Otter headed northward, flying for almost two hours up the rugged Labrador coastline. Below us, almost every bay held a grounded iceberg, some fresh and jagged, others softly rounded by months or even years of constant erosion by the elements. And beyond them, out in the deeper waters, were other icebergs, floating free, a silent fleet drifting down the coast. Further north, the land soon became dominated by the Torngat Mountains, rising some 1500 metres above the sea, their peaks still snow covered in midsummer. Broad U-shaped valleys, which were once filled with glacial ice, nestled between the peaks. In some, we could see small, round lakes and tall waterfalls that hung like white veils. Out at sea, the skies were clear and sunny, but inland, heavy storm clouds brooded over the Torngats and curtains of rain drew criss-cross patterns of light and dark among the valleys and mountain tops.

Banking westward, we turned into Nachvak Fiord, flying between the great pillars of rock that frame the entrance. On our right was Mount Razorback, once described as the most beautiful peak in northern Labrador, its rocky crags towering more than 1 000 metres and its saw-toothed ridge running parallel to the fiord for nearly six kilometres. At the end of the fiord, almost fifty kilometres inland from the Atlantic, we made a smooth landing on the glassy surface of a large

bay. Weather permitting, we would have just three days to camp, explore, and film.

The Torngats were named — with good reason — after the Inuit god of wind and storm. Climbers had warned us that strong winds could suddenly sweep down from the mountains, reaching speeds of 160 kilometres an hour, and we took care pitching our tent, tying the corners out to heavy boulders and lashing extra ropes to the peak. But our precautions proved unnecessary. The fierce spirit said to guard the Torngats paid no particular attention to us, and we enjoyed three days of warm summer weather in a perfect wilderness setting.

The temperature was close to twenty-four degrees Celsius, and at least five million blackflies shared the campsite with us. There were other visitors, too. A line of huge wolf tracks ran close to the water's edge, and late that first evening we heard a familiar sound — the explosive "whoosh" of a whale. It was a small minke, exploring the calm waters of the bay all by itself. An even better sound was the one we woke up to the next morning: two tundra wolves were serenading us from the hills about a kilometre from camp.

Some distance further down the beach was an area where the grasses and vegetation grew thick and green in contrast to the grey lichens and brown mosses on the surrounding tundra. It was the telltale sign of early human habitation, the clue that archeologists look for when they search for old Inuit settlement sites. This was the remains of a Thule Inuit winter house, perhaps 400 years old, and the lush green grasses grew where decaying refuse from the past had provided rich nutrients to the thin soil. The tent house would have been partly subterranean, the roof made from whalebone rafters covered with caribou skins and the floor fashioned from rock slabs. All that remained now was the deep depression in the ground and a few huge chunks of whalebone, some of them still forming part of the long entrance tunnel. Immediately above the house site, on top of a steep slope, were several piles of rock. We climbed up, startling a magnificent bull caribou, and peered in among the boulders. Inside, white bones gleamed in the dim light — human bones. These were the simple graves of families who had lived and died beside Nachvak Fiord a very long time ago.

The Inuit of the old Thule culture must have been tough and efficient hunters to have lived in such a raw and remote land. Because their chief prey was sea mammals, they stayed near the coast, exposed to the constant extremes of weather and the dangers of shifting pack ice. They wintered around the inner islands and coastal fiords, moving out early in the spring to hunt harp seals on the ice floes. Then, in summer, they dispersed in family groups to the outer islands to catch fish, waterfowl, and a variety of seals. Sometimes they made long voyages to trade with other Inuit groups. One of their trade items was Labrador chert, a hard mineral containing quartz and high-grade silica. They mined the chert at Ramah Bay, not far south from the entrance to Nachvak Fiord, and fashioned it into knives, tools, and spear points. Chert was a highly prized trade item, and it changed hands many times up and down the coast, turning up in regions as far south as New England. Although the land and the sea gave the Inuit most of what they needed, life could not have been easy.

Following the bull caribou we had startled on the hillside, we came to a wide, shallow bay where the air seemed warmer and the blackflies definitely more attentive. On the shore was a small group of caribou being driven almost insane by the biting hordes. These caribou were part of the George River herd, one of the largest caribou herds in Canada. Three bulls, with antlers bigger than any we had seen in the north Yukon, were running frantically into the water, trying to escape their tormentors. They stood in the shallows and shook, violent shudders coursing through their bodies, then came charging back out and galloped up and down the beach like race horses in training. Safely inside our headnets and protected by bug jackets heavily impregnated with oil of citronella, we watched and sympathized with the caribou. Relief for the caribou would soon come with the change of weather: bone-chilling storms are common in summer. Meanwhile, they suffered on.

The isolated splendour and untouched wilderness of the Torngats has made this region a natural candidate for national park status. The first tentative boundary lines were being sketched in on maps while we were in Nain; however, no decisions had been made about when or if a national park might be created here. For climbers who have come to these mountains, the experience has had a profound effect upon them. In their journals and diaries, they have written some of the most vivid descriptions of Labrador; from the hazardous boat trip up the coast, to the heady exhilaration of reaching Mont D'Iberville, the highest peak on Canada's eastern mainland.

Nature has protected the Torngats well. These inland fiords and mountains are hard places to reach, and once you are there, the feeling of distance and isolation becomes very real. As yet, there are no roads or scheduled air flights into the Torngat region so travel remains costly and difficult, with the weather always playing the determining role. Our three days among the Torngats permitted us to glimpse the very character of northern Labrador, an immense land of endless granite rock, of sea and ice — a land whose very remoteness has allowed it to remain one of the last truly wild places left in North America.

CHAPTER SIX

HIGH ARCTIC JOURNEY

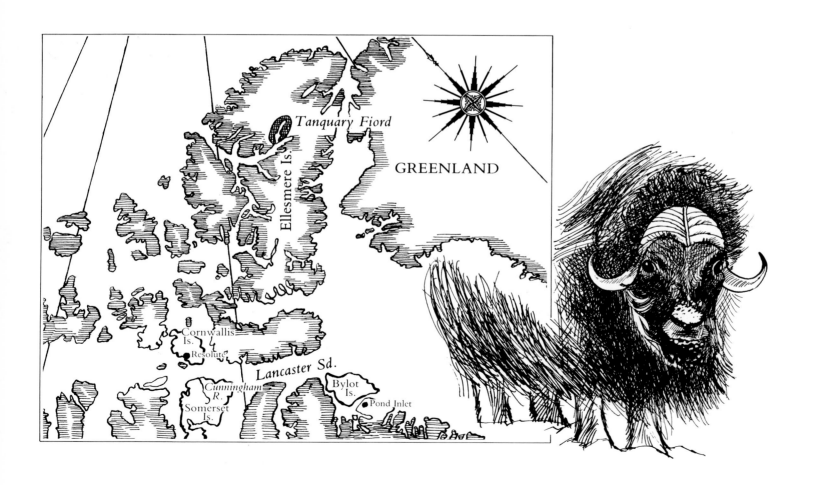

WE WERE STILL CURLED UP in thick sleeping-bags when the melody began. A new sound had drifted through the valley and lingered now in our sleepy subconscious. Awakening slowly, we strained to hear beyond the light flapping of the cotton tent and the occasional liquid cry of a ruddy turnstone. Then it came again — a high-pitched song of arctic freedom that reaches into your soul like no other sound on earth. On a steep ridge, about a kilometre from camp, a single white arctic wolf was serenading our tent.

At once the inside of the tent turned into a wild confusion of thrashing sleeping-bags, flying clothing, and hands reaching for boots and cameras. Nothing sticks like the front zipper of a tent when you are in a hurry, and nothing disappears faster than the pair of socks so carefully placed the night before. Nevertheless, we made it outside in record time, boots in one hand, binoculars in the other. Quickly we scanned the ridge and saw the wolf immediately. He was beautifully rim-lit in the polar sun, a halo of white fur gleaming against the old grey rock. Staring back at us through the tundra's shimmering ground haze, he raised his head to howl once more. For a long moment we watched and listened in wonder as his song died away among the ice floes and hanging glaciers of Tanquary Fiord. If you are moved by wilderness and wild things, there is nothing quite so exciting as being howled at by an arctic wolf.

Here was an animal that was everything we were not. He lived freely and competently in the harsh arctic environment, whereas we had to carry a complete life support system with us, or risk death from starvation and exposure. The laws governing his life were very different from ours. To survive, an arctic wolf must hunt across many hundreds of square kilometres in all seasons, searching for a meal among the scattered and fleet-footed little bands of arctic creatures, or scavenging for carrion and other edible odds and ends. Not an easy way to live. But this was July, and he was probably enjoying the least difficult time of his year — the brief and vibrant arctic summer.

Lying full length, with his nose between his paws like a dog in front of a fire-place, the wolf continued to examine us from his vantage point on the ridge. He sniffed the unfamiliar smell of our camp and was obviously curious. Perhaps he had never seen a human before. Curious or not, it was evident that he was not coming down for a closer look.

Meanwhile, we were trying to figure out how to get closer to him. We would be in plain view all the way. I remembered the laughing advice of Bill Mason, who had spent months trying to shoot close-ups of wolves. "There's no way," he had said. "You just can't sneak up on a wolf." Still, it was worth a try. Counting on the wolf's inquisitive nature, we gathered up tripods, film gear, and long lenses and moved out toward the ridge. The animal sat up immediately, watching as we stumbled through the tussock tundra. As we drew nearer to a now very alert wolf, we tried to line ourselves up so that he would see only one person at a time, in the faint hope that this might make a difference. About fifty metres from the rise, I hissed at Janet to stop. "I'm going to try for a long shot." Lowering the tripod, I bedded down the legs securely into the ground and swung the sixteen millimetre camera and telephoto lens toward the wolf. Or where he was. He had slipped away. Janet promptly began to howl, giving the best imitation she could in the hope that he would stay in the area for one more look. Her howl is an almost perfect imitation of a southern Ontario coyote's and has frequently produced spectacular results on our farm. One can only imagine the surprise the wolf must have felt on hearing from a southern cousin at the north end of Ellesmere Island.

We ran for the ridge. Although badly out of breath, we were urged on by the excitement that builds when you are sure that a major wildlife encounter is near. Too hurriedly, we stuck our heads above the rocks. He was there all right, gazing at us with glowing amber eyes, and then whipping away smartly as six tripod legs hit the ground. No, you can't sneak up on a wolf, but even a glimpse is reward enough. Ten minutes later, we saw not one but two wolves trotting away on long white legs, continuing their circuit of the hills and valleys beyond Tanquary Fiord, and always just out of camera range.

After the wolves had left, we sat above the valley and rested, binoculars slowly sweeping the majestic scenery. To the north, the Grant Land Mountains began. Ancient glacial ice flowed down between the peaks and spread out on level ground in crystal pools, the immense and neatly rounded walls of each glacier almost touching one another on the valley floor. Between the ridge and the mountains, the MacDonald River swiftly carried away meltwater, braiding its way through the gravel and chewing at the far bank where several tonnes of soil and debris fell as we watched. To the east, a superb system of valleys and glaciers beckoned. Somewhere just beyond them lay Hazen Lake, seventy-eight kilometres long and up to eleven kilometres wide, the largest body of fresh water in the high polar regions.

Behind us to the south-west, the land sloped gently down to Tanquary Fiord and our campsite. As in most ecosystems, water is life in the Arctic; the tiny stream that gurgled into the fiord near our camp was a magnet for many species of animals and plants. Dwarf willows, a favourite food of the arctic hare, spread vigorously over the damp ground, their pinkish flowering pods standing upright above the dark leaves. Exquisite mounds of purple saxifrage hugged the stony tundra, staying low to keep out of the arctic wind. Nearby, bright clusters of arctic poppies bobbed and swayed with each gust of wind, their flowers tracking the summer sun like little solar receivers. At the outer limits of ten-power binoculars, we spotted a snowy owl, perched on a lichen-crusted boulder beside the stream and nearly lost in the almost liquid ground haze that often frustrates long-distance photography.

A scattering of arctic hares came into view, perhaps a dozen of them, hopping among pools of water trapped by permafrost and eating every flower they could find. They too were white, ridiculously white against the soft greens and browns of summer, obvious targets for predators. Only the young ones, which scampered

Long-tailed jaegers are spectacular fliers. These were hovering and balancing on a strong wind. A wide-angle lens
caught them at close range.

Four o'clock in the morning at Alexandra Fiord, on the east side of Ellesmere Island. Three ducks have just paddled over to visit a family of snow geese.

fearlessly around our tent, were born with a sensible natural colouring that must give them some protection from owls, foxes, and wolves. But by winter they would also be white.

We moved slowly toward the adult hares. They were so easy to photograph that we could wait for the right light, find the best background, and take the time to capture the most interesting behaviour. These are the largest hares in North America; a full-grown adult is usually heavier than an arctic fox. And although they appear to be easy targets, the fox that goes after them will soon find itself involved in some high-speed running. As a natural consequence of life in open country, they have learned to run and hop alternately so that they can switch, at top speed, from a four-legged run to a two-legged hop, without slowing down. By rising up on their hind legs and hopping furiously, they are able to take a good look around for danger. While doing this, they look like small white kangaroos.

We started back toward camp and breakfast, invigorated by the clear morning, the hike, and the wildlife encounters — and accompanied for part of the way by an irritated long-tailed jaeger with strong views about whose territory this was. Jaegers defending nesting territory hover above the intruder and then dive, screaming like banshees as they flash by. This behaviour indicates that a nest is near, and it is best to walk on carefully until the dive-bombing stops. The nest, which is little more than a depression in the ground, and the well-camouflaged eggs are so difficult to see that you literally have to watch every step. The same care must be taken when passing through the territory of a black-bellied plover or a ruddy turnstone. At this latitude, where summer is extremely short, the birds may have only one opportunity to

This great shaggy head seemed to rise up suddenly out of the tundra. We did not realize it then, but a solitary bull muskox can be dangerous.

A frightening moment. Would the muskox charge again?

nest and rear their young. Predation, or a major disturbance that drives them off their territory, may mean that there will be no time for them to try again. Not every photographer realizes that a successful search for a nest also leaves a scent trail, which may be picked up and followed by the next predator to pass by.

It was while we were tiptoeing through the jaeger's territory and looking up to take pictures that I

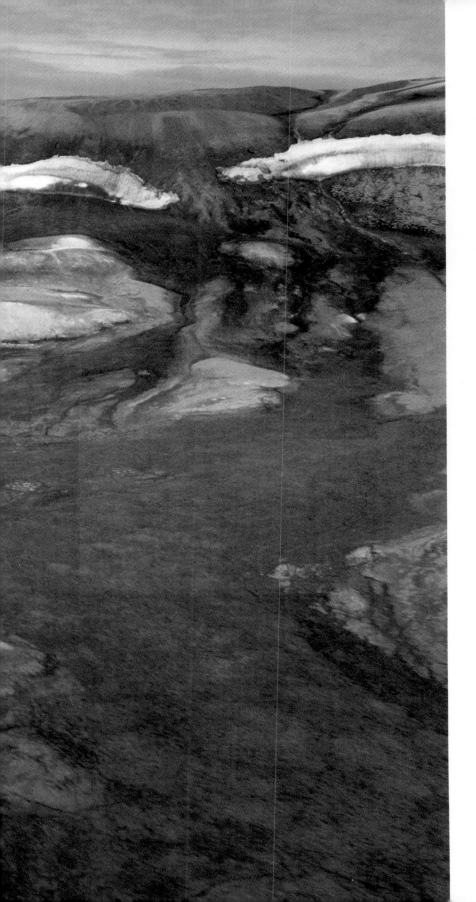

ABOVE   *Adult arctic hares on Ellesmere Island. Sometimes they can be found in groups of several hundred.*

LEFT   *A classic arctic oasis. The sedge meadows and grasses are fed by the banks of melting snow and sheltered by the confines of the valley. These are precious pools of life for wild creatures in a harsh land. Note small group of musk-oxen at upper left on green slope.*

ABOVE   *Another perfect campsite — at the head of Tanquary*
Fiord on Ellesmere Island.

OPPOSITE   *This Ellesmere Island glacier is unusually well*
defined. To us, it looked like a river frozen suddenly as it
spilled out of the hills.

unexpectedly found myself face to face with a shaggy head peering over the top of a muddy depression. Like the Ancient Mariner, a large male muskox had fixed us with a glittering eye. He appeared to be neither aggressive nor afraid. A few snorts and rumbles came our way as he began to bunt the soft soil beside him with one of his wickedly curved horns. We stood quietly, about twelve metres away, taking photographs. Several minutes later, his behaviour changed slightly. He now appeared to be rubbing his nose on one front leg. Still unaware that some very explicit body language was coming our way, I began to move slowly around him, speaking softly and keeping a careful distance, but paying little attention to the two gleaming eyes that tracked me over the tundra. The muskox continued to dig out the soil and to breathe heavily. It should be explained here that muskoxen, which are loosely related to sheep and goats, are amazingly swift and nimble-footed, in spite of their ungainly appearance. Secondly, as I was to learn, solitary bulls are known to be irritable, unpredictable, and dangerous. Thirdly, we had been around him much too long and were too close. These factors now combined, and the muskox exploded into action.

All I remember was a rumble of hooves and a blur of brown fury moving in my direction. Desperately, I turned and tried to leap across a wide, water-filled depression. Predictably, I landed in the middle and was instantly swept off my feet by the smooth layer of ice beneath the water. I landed face down, about as terrified as I had ever been in my life. (Janet said later that I had "flown through the air." With something less than wifely concern, she had the good sense to continue photographing.) As I scrambled out of the ditch, the muskox calmly surveyed me from the other side, apparently satisfied with the spectacular results of his charge. It had been a false charge, which

had achieved its purpose beautifully. I was soaked, my camera was leaking water from somewhere inside, and, perhaps worst of all, a precious roll of exposed film had dropped out of my pocket and now lay within snorting distance of the muskox. I gave up any intention of reclaiming it. Slowly and cautiously, we retrieved our packs and tripods and backed away, Janet happy to see that I was still intact, but happier, I suspect, to have recorded the event on film. The muskox guarded my roll of film and made low, growling sounds as we moved off into safer country.

Weeks later, I telephoned Dr. David Gray at Canada's National Museum of Natural Sciences to find out what the muskox had been trying to tell us. "You were probably just too close, or perhaps he had just been defeated in a fight," he said, "and they are somewhat belligerent when solitary. In fact, it's far more dangerous to face a solitary bull than a herd which has gone into its defensive circle." He went on to analyse the bull's behaviour. What we had witnessed, just before the charge, were two clear warnings. The first one was "horning" — the muskox using one horn to dig at the soil beside him. The second was "gland-rubbing." To our eyes this appeared to be nothing more than the animal rubbing the side of his nose on one foreleg. There was much more to it than that. A small gland on the cheek-bone just below the eye secretes a fluid when rubbed, emitting a scent that communicates aggressive intentions. Humans cannot smell this scent, but other muskoxen can. These two forms of behaviour, gland rubbing and horning, are generally used to attract another muskox's attention, and to give the rival animal a chance to respond or clear out. When we failed to read these signals and to back off, the muskox attacked.

I escaped with a flooded camera and a good soaking in icy water. Because I was only a half-hour from

RIGHT *The mysterious narwhal, source of the legend of the unicorn.*

BELOW *Beluga whales at Cunningham Inlet. This photograph was taken from the research scientists' observation tower.*

A brief moment of beauty as the midnight sun touches drifting ice floes in Pond Inlet.

camp, the wet clothing was less serious than it might have been, given the uncertainties of arctic weather. But the experience did illustrate an interesting point about dressing for a cool climate. I was wearing a parka insulated with one of the new synthetic fibres. I had chosen the parka deliberately, knowing that down-filled clothing is useless when wet. The down goes into little wet lumps and takes forever to dry. But the synthetic fibres, although bulkier, will not retain moisture. Even as I backed away from the muskox, the water was running out of my parka. In fact, although all of my clothing underneath was wet, I kept the parka on because its insulating qualities were still intact. Things were a bit clammy for a while, but I was protected from the cold winds and relatively warm.

Back at camp, we stepped carefully around three young arctic hares nibbling flowers at the edge of Tanquary Fiord, greeted the apparently solitary long-tailed jaeger perched on the tent, and turned our thoughts to breakfast. After frying up some bannock and sharing it with the jaeger, we sat back and wondered what else the day could possibly bring. We wondered, too, about the future of this extraordinary place. Tanquary Fiord would soon be attracting attention as the focal point for a new High Arctic national park. A reserve of over 40 000 square kilometres had just been announced, a vast wedge-shaped area taking in not only the pristine valleys leading inland from the fiord, but also the great range of mountains that extend to the polar seas at the northern rim of North America. East of these mountains the park reserve continues, embracing Lake Hazen and the Hazen Plateau, and reaching across to the Robeson Channel, a narrow stretch of water separating Ellesmere Island from Greenland.

However, the creation of a national park here will not be without controversy. Serious concerns have

The Canadian Coast Guard ship Franklin *in Pond Inlet.*
To the north are the mountains and glaciers of Bylot Island.

Mid-August on the south coast of Devon Island. These cliffs stand along the northern edge of Lancaster Sound. A dusting of snow was a sharp reminder that the short arctic summer was coming to an end.

been raised about the impact of large numbers of visitors on this most delicate and northern of all arctic environments. To understand this, it is interesting to reflect for a moment on the impact of our own little expedition. We had attempted to photograph an arctic wolf, inadvertently irritated a solitary bull muskox to the point of charging, and entered the nesting territory of several species of birds, including the sensitive jaeger. No doubt we had trampled many tiny arctic flowers, although we did try to watch where we put our feet. All of this was done innocently enough; we are both very aware of the possibilities for ecological disruption in such a place.

Now multiply our activities to the tune of three or four hundred tourists a year. Understand that they may not realize how their own activities could possibly cause any harm. Naturally, they will want to see the scenery, the flowers, and the wildlife, and because they have spent a great deal of money to get to Tanquary Fiord for their arctic adventure, they will also be anxious to cover as much ground as possible. Out across the tundra they will go, through the brief and precious arctic summer. Perhaps a small hotel will be built at the head of the fiord. Such a proposal exists. Perhaps, too, limited hunting will be permitted for the Inuit. Suddenly, everything will change. What will this once pristine arctic lowland look like in ten years? Will there be any muskoxen, arctic hares, wolves, or snowy owls? Will tourists have worn trails into the tundra and damaged plant communities that could take twenty years to recover? The simple truth is that even a modest amount of tourism in such a place is going to have a very large impact.

Why is the area so vulnerable? First, you have to look at the conditions that dominate life here. Northern Ellesmere is a polar desert receiving, in many areas, less precipitation than the Sahara Desert. Near Lake Hazen, for example, the entire year's precipitation, including snow, measures only two or three centimetres. Throughout most of the year, it is intensely cold, with dry winds and little snow cover to protect plants. These conditions impose severe restrictions on plant and animal life, which can thrive only in the relatively rich lowlands, where there is moisture, shelter, soil, and slightly warmer conditions. But only a tiny percentage of the High Arctic enjoys these conditions. Thus, the lowlands are vital for the survival of the region's mammals, birds, insects, and plants, which have few, if any, other options. As an increasing number of people go north to the Arctic, the clash between animals and man will become even more serious. Visitors invariably want to head for the shelter of valleys where there is fine scenery, water, and such an abundance of life that they may get the mistaken impression that the arctic islands are full of wildlife. As a result, some animals may be slowly forced out of important territory. Unable to survive in the arid areas or up on the exposed, lifeless slopes, they will have to search for new range, away from human disturbance, if they can find it.

If visitation can be spread out thinly, or carefully controlled in the most sensitive areas, and if activities such as hunting are strictly prohibited, it will be possible to create a national park here that will retain two of its reasons for existence: to provide a true arctic experience only a few hundred kilometres from the North Pole, and to protect another unique segment of the Canadian landscape. This will take some courageous and determined planning in the face of political pressures to create a tourism industry in the High Arctic as quickly as possible.

A week of filming and exploring on northern Ellesmere Island was coming to an end. It was time to move a long way south, to an inlet at the mouth of the Cunningham River on Somerset Island, where several hundred beluga whales (also called white whales) should be gathering. We had been told by radio that an aircraft would make a brief stop at Tanquary Fiord to pick us up. Janet and I broke camp, and then sat by the radio with one worried eye on the weather system that was descending rapidly from the mountains. As the pilot tried to thread his way among the hills and valleys between our camp and Lake Hazen, we could hear him reporting deteriorating conditions to his base 900 kilometres away at Resolute. By now, there were no hills in sight to the east of us — only cloud and mist. We reported our weather to the pilot and continued to wait. Visitors can be stuck for a long time in one place in the Arctic, isolated by bad weather or by the absence of passing aircraft.

We were lucky to be officially plugged into a unique Canadian organization that makes it possible for hundreds of scientists and researchers to move about this truly immense part of the world. It is called the Polar Continental Shelf Project and is an arm of Energy, Mines and Resources, a federal government department. Known to most people simply as Polar Shelf, it provides logistical support for the many scientists, biologists, archaeologists, park planners, geologists, and people from every conceivable academic discipline who are doing serious work in the Arctic. All of this costs a great deal of money, and without the help of Polar Shelf, most would be unable to pursue their projects. This would be a loss to science and to Canada. Polar Shelf is generous with its help, providing millions of dollars worth of flying time, fuel, equipment, and even food and lodging while the scientists are in Resolute. However, frivolous or scientifically unsound proposals are unlikely to pass the

scrutiny of the scientific advisors who examine each project. Supported by our film budget, and with considerable help from both Polar Shelf and Parks Canada, we were able to fly to our filming locations on the Twin Otter aircraft and Jet Ranger helicopters that hurry in and out of Resolute sometimes twenty-four hours a day.

If Polar Shelf said to us, "We will pick you up at your camp at 4:30 in the morning and move you over to Alexandra Fiord," we would be sitting on our packs, ready to go, at 4:30. Each field party is supplied with a powerful short wave radio tuned to the Polar Shelf frequency and must report in at a pre-arranged time, twice a day. A portable weather station and precise training on how to use it are also provided. Although the latest in satellite pictures and other forms of weather technology are received by the base every day, there is no substitute for the person on the ground looking at the sky. The twice-daily radio "sched" between field parties and Polar Shelf's base at Resolute or Tuktoyaktuk is taken very seriously: miss two consecutively scheduled radio checks and an aircraft is sent out to look for you — at your expense. It is an interesting experience to sit in the Polar Shelf radio shack at Resolute listening to the crackling voices coming in from many hundreds of kilometres away in all directions, their positions marked on a huge map of the arctic islands. Like a benevolent but strict guardian, Polar Shelf must listen to problems, issue orders, send out fuel and supplies, fly people from one distant island to another, worry about the weather, and provide hot showers, food, and beds for groups that come and go — all the while operating what amounts to an arctic airline. A dozen helicopters and a pair of Twin Otters, leased from private companies, are constantly on the move and frequently landing in strange and difficult places. The Otters, which have a short take-off and landing capability, are fitted with large, fat, low-pressure tires — generally known as "tundra tires." If the ground is reasonably firm, more or less level, and free from large boulders or deep depressions, you may find yourself bouncing in for a tundra tire landing where no aircraft has landed before.

All of this activity is tightly co-ordinated on a daily basis from Resolute. Without such an organization, not only would scientists find it far more difficult to cover the forbidding distances and to cope with the sometimes terrible weather conditions of the arctic islands, but also far less would be known today about the Arctic's resources, landforms, ocean currents, ice conditions, geology, history, wildlife, and weather. The Polar Continental Shelf Project was founded in 1958, in response to an urgent need for more information about the continental shelf surrounding the arctic islands. Today, largely through the efforts of Polar Shelf, Canada possesses a large body of knowledge about the islands and exerts its sovereignty over them with a friendly scientific army of occupation.

The Twin Otter whispered in along the walls of Tanquary Fiord and had begun to bank for a landing before we even heard it. We grabbed the radio and asked the pilot to go round again, "just for the camera." Good-naturedly, he agreed, standing the Otter on one wing low over the fiord's pack ice. We laughed when a distant voice from Resolute, where our transmissions had been monitored, broke in and said, "I hope you've got your silk scarf streaming out the window!"

Forty minutes later we were in the air heading south for Resolute on Cornwallis Island. As the pilot gained altitude, he reached down and punched some numbers into a computer mounted on the instrument panel.

These were the co-ordinates giving the precise position of Resolute. Once they are locked into the computer's memory, low-frequency signals from ground stations are constantly monitored by the computer, compared with the co-ordinates, and matched against wind speed, wind direction, air speed, time, and distance. Corrections are made every few seconds. All of this information is visible on a simple instrument in front of the pilot and lets him know if he is flying to the right or left of his course. The system saves money and fuel, especially in bad weather. George Hobson, Director of Polar Shelf, says it's "the pilot's piece of string that leads him home."

Having set his course, the pilot now leaned forward and peered through a device, which looked to us like an ancient sextant, mounted in front of the windshield. It was, in fact, a sun compass. Like an early explorer in a tiny sailboat, he was double-checking his position by taking a shot of the sun. We found this combination of high technology and ancient navigational techniques somewhat hilarious, particularly the pilot's polite mistrust of his fancy computer. Every pilot has a style, a way of flying that is based on experience. One arctic pilot, legendary for his skills with the Twin Otter, refers to his computer as "plastic brains" and refuses to use it. He knows where he is going.

An ordinary magnetic compass would be useless at these latitudes — for very good reasons. The compass, which normally swings along magnetic lines of force and points to the North Magnetic Pole, runs into problems here, because it is simply too close to the Magnetic Pole, and is being pulled downward instead of from side to side. As you approach the North Magnetic Pole, the lines of force point down into the earth, and the compass needle tries to follow. The result is a compass that is trying to stand on its head — not a very reliable instrument in these circumstances. Even if the compass did point steadily to the North Magnetic Pole, it would still lack precision, for the pole is an area rather than a point. Indeed, the closer the compass gets to the pole, the more inaccurate it becomes, and anyone trying to steer for the pole itself would probably miss it by a wide margin. The main reason for this is that the North Magnetic Pole is actually wandering around. Every day it moves through an ellipse of 193 by 40 kilometres and the ellipse itself moves about 7 kilometres every ten years. Thus, it would be impossible to establish an accurate system of magnetic bearings from one point to another, because it would become useless within hours.

Following our electronic piece of string, we flew south across the elemental splendour of Ellesmere Island, over domes of ice blending into the sky, and past inlets and fiords reaching deep into the land. Land and water stretched away on all sides, farther than the eye could see even from several thousand metres. Such is the scale of this part of our globe that we could not help feeling a sense of isolation from the rest of North America. From here, the southern mainland seemed strangely distant, and somehow diminished in size and importance. First-time arctic travellers often experience these sensations. A look at a map beforehand (if one can be found that includes all of the arctic islands) does not prepare you for the reality of the distances involved or the immensity of the islands themselves. Perhaps these sensations and discoveries are part of the polar passion, part of the reason that many arctic visitors feel the need to return again and again.

Trailing a boiling column of dust, the Twin Otter turned off the wide gravel strip at Resolute and taxied over to the humble little building that houses the Polar Shelf radio communications equipment. We unloaded our gear and went inside to listen to the evening radio "sched," hoping to hear news from the two scientists who were waiting for beluga whales at a river estuary on Somerset Island. The news was good: several hundred of the beautiful white whales had entered the bay and were now close to the mouth of the Cunningham River.

We spoke briefly by radio to Wybrand Hoek, a marine mammal technician from the federal government's Arctic Biological Station at Ste. Anne de Bellevue, and to Dr. Tom Smith, a research scientist studying behaviour and communication patterns of the beluga whales. They gave us permission to camp with them and to use their observation platform to film the whales, provided our filming did not disturb the animals. We were advised to bring hip-waders for crossing the channels at the edge of the tidal estuary, and a rifle for scaring away polar bears. A couple of years earlier, at the same location, a scientist had been attacked by a bear and dragged away by his head. He was saved by a colleague with a rifle. We had no desire to be responsible for the death of a bear, so we had also brought some impressive noisemakers. From the Canadian Navy we had obtained a dozen "thunderflashes," enormous firecrackers about the size of railway flares and with ten-second fuses. We also had an old twelve-gauge British Army flare pistol, which makes a loud noise and sends out a large red ball of light. It could be used at longer range.

We had absolutely no idea what a hungry polar bear would think of all this firepower; our hope was to drive it away before it came too close. Once a polar bear is within a hundred metres of you, there is the very real danger of a sudden charge with little time to react. The 30.06 rifle was a final defence. As before, when working in grizzly country in the north Yukon, we kept the rifle unloaded and a full clip of cartridges ready in a pocket. Many arctic researchers carry a short shot-gun, loaded with slugs, which is useless at long range. The point is that serious trouble will happen only at close range. This removes the temptation to pick off a distant bear because you are afraid it will come closer. The death of an innocent bear that is simply reacting to an intruder in its territory, or investigating a messy camp, is always a tragedy. Every arctic traveller should carry noisemakers and know how and when to use the rifle.

The summer migration of beluga whales into the shallow river estuaries of the arctic islands is a phenomenon that has been noted and recorded from the earliest days of arctic exploration. Regrettably, it inspired greed rather than wonder in the minds of those European explorers. Thousands of these sleek, intelligent marine mammals were subsequently slaughtered by commercial whalers, who came to hunt bowhead whales but turned to white whales as a supplementary source of oil. Although the European whalers eventually stopped hunting in the Arctic, local whaling continued.

Unfortunately, belugas are easy to kill. Driven by powerful, ancient instincts, they return year after year to the same river mouths. Once in shallow water, they are easy to herd with fast boats and have little chance against experienced hunters. The World Wildlife Fund of Canada, alarmed by the decline of arctic whale species, raised three-quarters of a million dollars in 1982 for arctic whale research, with the intention of enhancing our knowledge and improving our management of these ancient mammals of the sea. The Cunningham Inlet population is one group being studied. The belugas entering this inlet each summer

A De Havilland Twin Otter, the workhorse of the High Arctic, comes down on a typically rough landing strip. Tundra tires mounted on DC-3 wheels help to soften the shock of landing.

probably winter off the west coast of Greenland. They are part of a population of about 10 000 white whales that travel into Lancaster Sound each spring. The isolation of the Cunningham River estuary, and its distance from settlements, make it an ideal place to study an undisturbed population of whales for a few weeks in the summer. Because the whales may panic at the sound of an engine, much of the work is done by observers on shore and from a six-metre aluminum tower.

The pilots of passing aircraft, who might normally be tempted to drop down for a closer look at hundreds of belugas in one bay, give the river mouth a wide berth while the scientists are at work. As we approached the inlet in the Twin Otter, our pilot began a turn that would bring us toward the camp from the south instead of over the river from the north. We were still above the deep waters of Barrow Strait when he began his turn, and as the airplane banked, we found ourselves looking directly down into the blue depths of the Northwest Passage. From her front seat perch, Janet remarked on the patterns of ice floes against the dark water. Then she looked again. "Wait a minute," she shouted above the roar of the Otter, "those aren't ice floes, they're whales!" And indeed they were, gleaming white in the summer sun, jewels in a rich blue sea. They appeared to be right on course for the Cunningham River.

Once again the tundra tires bounced and shook along the surface of an air strip provided by nature. The research camp was located over a kilometre from the bay where the whales were gathering, but even from this distance the bay appeared to be speckled with white-caps. Squeaks, whistles, grunts, and an extraordinary variety of other sounds floated faintly through the still air. Later, quietly sitting in Tom Smith's observation tower on the end of a long gravel bar at the edge of the bay, we waited for the rising tide to bring the whales into a channel directly below us. They moved in swiftly, sometimes in groups creating bow waves ahead of them. Calves swam easily above their mothers' backs, carried in the slip-streams like little cars behind big trucks. Some whales seemed to turn their heads and look up at us through the clear water as they swam by. For a few priceless hours, we were being given a window into the private world of the belugas.

Around the fringes of the bay, whales were lying in shallow water, their tail flukes arched high in the air. Clearly they were scratching themselves on the gravel bars, adding more weight to the theory that these river estuaries are vital for moulting. As Wybrand Hoek said later, "It's a great place to come for a scratch!" When the whales arrive, they are a yellowish colour, but when they leave, they are a gleaming white, having moulted and rubbed off the outer layer of old skin. Other whales swam for long periods with their heads held high enough out of the water for their eyes to clear the surface. Two or three would spy-hop together, apparently having a good look around. And while they rubbed and rolled and splashed, the bay was filled with sounds.

Part of the investigation here is a study of the vocalization patterns of belugas. The scientists spend many cold hours in their tower, quietly speaking into a tape recorder and describing whale behaviour, while underwater microphones simultaneously record the voices of the whales. It may take many seasons of this kind of work before accurate conclusions can be reached about the cacophony of sounds reaching the microphones. One researcher compared the complex repertoire of the beluga whale to "an orchestra tuning up." The variability and number of whistles alone is thought to be very significant. Imagine trying to relate the whistles, clicks, snores, grunts, and the sophisticated pulsing sounds — literally packages of energy emitted in groups — to the specific behaviour of one whale or group of whales at a certain moment, and you will be able to glimpse the difficulties in attempting to penetrate the beluga's language. However, if the Cunningham Inlet scientists are successful, the results of their experiments will be a valuable addition to the store of knowledge slowly being accumulated in an effort to initiate better understanding and management of the species.

Although commercial whaling of belugas has officially ended, at least three arctic and sub-arctic populations continue to decline because of hunting pressure from local native communities. Today, the whale is prized only for its muktuk, the outer layer of skin.

The rest of the carcass is left on the beach, unless there are dogs to feed. Muktuk has long been considered a rich country food, a delicacy to be shared with the whole community. But there are fewer whales now and larger questions. The crash of one population — a real possibility — will add weight to the world-wide criticism of Canada's arctic whaling policies. The Inuit are becoming increasingly aware that such criticism may have an effect on their rights to continue hunting the land of their ancestors. However, because whaling is one small part of the larger, long-standing issue of land claims and aboriginal rights, it is essential to apply sensible conservation laws acceptable to all while the larger controversies are being resolved. When wildlife is caught in the middle, it can suffer from the half-hearted regulation of hunting activities. Scientists and wildlife managers would like to cut through the political red tape and work with native communities in applying mutually acceptable quotas, sound management practices, and complete protection when necessary to allow a population to recover. There will, of course, always be the emotional question of whether all whaling should be ended. To some, this is also a moral question, a question of whether man has the right to kill such apparently intelligent animals.

In addition to concern about the beluga populations, there is growing worry about the other small arctic whale — the legendary sea unicorn or narwhal. This mottled, silvery grey-black mammal, about four to six metres long, was hunted for nearly 1000 years by early explorers and commercial whalers. Its spiralled tusk inspired many incredible tales. Throughout Europe, "the horn of the unicorn" was assigned magical properties by the whalers. Whalers returning home to European ports with shiploads of tusks deliberately added to the beliefs and legends. Their stories of the fierce unicorn were so convincing that the real origin of the tusk was concealed for centuries. Many Europeans came to believe in the existence of a four-legged, strangely built, and dangerous land mammal, with a tusk in the centre of its forehead. Few would have guessed that this fabulous "tusk" was actually the greatly elongated tooth of a sea mammal, a tooth that sometimes reaches three metres in length.

There has been considerable debate as to the purpose of the narwhal's tusk. Some people believe it is used to stir up the sea floor while the animal is searching for food. Others think it may be useful for breaking ice at the surface for breathing holes, or to impale arctic cod. We saw two narwhals with their tusks conveniently propped up on an ice floe as they rested. What is generally accepted is that the tusk is a male characteristic for display purposes. However, it is also known to be used in aggressive encounters between males, and many carry scars to prove it. The tip of a broken-off tusk has sometimes been discovered embedded in the flesh of a male narwhal. The occurrence of broken tusks has led the noted arctic traveller and writer, Fred Bruemmer, to speculate that these animals "may have a ten-foot toothache."

Narwhals have followed their migratory routes into the Canadian Arctic for centuries, moving westward each summer from the seas around Greenland into Lancaster Sound. Originally they were hunted only by nomadic bands of Inuit, who were as migratory as the whales themselves. Long before the arrival of the Norsemen, the narwhal tusk was prized as a trade item between Inuit groups. However, their ability to kill large numbers must have been limited, and the recovery of harpooned animals may have been dangerous for men in small kayaks. With the establishment of Viking settlements in Greenland, in the tenth century, a new trade in ivory began, and the legend of the unicorn was born. In the years that followed, thousands of narwhals were hunted down by European whalers.

By the turn of this century, the Inuit of north Baffin Island were dependent on the trade in skins and ivory for their supplies of ammunition and tobacco, which they obtained from Scottish traders. The traders, in turn, depended on the hunters and ensured that they were sufficiently supplied with food for the spring narwhal hunt. In 1923 the Hudson's Bay Company managed to squeeze out its competitors in the north Baffin region; the narwhal, in the form of oil, ivory, and skin for gloves, continued to find its way to Europe. Today at Pond Inlet, the hunt continues, but on a much smaller scale. It is still largely a commercial hunt for ivory, although the muktuk is treasured as food by hunting families. Little use is made of the meat or blubber.

We flew noisily into Pond Inlet in an aged but perfectly operational DC-3 that makes a regular run from Resolute. Besides the six to seven hundred permanent residents of Pond Inlet, there was a typical summer influx of people from the south, including tourists in search of an arctic experience or on their way to fish for arctic char. Although the sun still shone twenty-four hours a day, July was coming to an end, and at midnight the sun dipped noticeably toward the mountains of Bylot Island. These mountains marching across the northern sky and tinged with purple, blue and white, provide the people of Pond Inlet with a spectacular view across the ice-choked waters separating Baffin from Bylot Island. It is a splendid setting for their hamlet. Frequently, massive icebergs float in from Baffin Bay. Gargantuan fragments of Greenland glaciers, they drift back and forth with wind and tide,

and sometimes run aground. One of these was firmly anchored just off shore. It had arrived almost a year ago and was only now beginning to break up.

After arranging for a room in the busy little hotel, we went in search of a boat that could take us out to the ice floes and perhaps to the grounded iceberg. Soon, with an experienced driver at the helm, we were threading our way through the drifting floes, looking hopefully among the channels for narwhals. The whales, however, are quickly scared away by the sound of outboard motors, and, in any case, the small boat was not a very good camera platform. We tested a few ice floes for stability, but they were moving too fast. The iceberg, which would have made a fine perch, was now far too dangerous. Later that day, it split in half with a sound like cannon fire, sending up a wave that would have swamped a small outboard. In spite of the spectacular scenery and fine weather, it was becoming obvious that filming narwhals was not going to be easy.

Nevertheless, there was plenty to see and photograph in Pond Inlet. The hamlet was in a holiday mood, preparing for a three-day week-end in glorious weather. This was high summer in a land that is dark throughout the winter. Down on the beach, the big, open, square-stern canoes were lined up and being filled to the gunwales with food, equipment, and families. The ubiquitous three-wheeled, balloon-tired motor cycles buzzed back and forth, some pulling loaded komatiks in an interesting blend of technology and tradition. Soft caribou skins and well-worn rifles lay beside rows of filled containers of gasoline — all waiting their turn to go aboard. Children pulled on warm outer clothing in readiness for a long, cold trip through the ice floes. It seemed as if all of Pond Inlet was going to camp. One after another the boats pulled away, taking hunters and families back to the land they love.

This link with the not-so-distant past is perhaps the strongest tie that the Inuit have with their origins. Although many of them are wage-earners rather than full-time hunters, every male Inuit and many of the women are considered to be hunters,and hunt at least part of the time. It is the most honourable profession; the outpost camp, where country food is available and the worries of life in town are forgotten, is a treasured part of their lives. One young hunter expressed it this way: "People here are very much a part of the environment because we live close with the land and the sea and its animals. Our pride, our very desire to live, is because of our closeness with the environment around us and the animals we can enjoy and harvest for food. Our culture depends on hunting and being able to roam freely. My joy is the animals and the land and the sea and the freedom that goes with it."

Those are strong, sincere, and passionate words from a people increasingly critical of southerners. The need to be a hunter, to know independence, is deeply felt. So, too, is the desire for wild food — indeed, this may be a physical as well as a spiritual need. But the move from the land into organized settlements was inevitable. Dwindling game populations, cold, and the risks of starvation accelerated the move. It was a time of upheaval and change that cut deeply into the heart of their culture. As one arctic traveller said, "they gave up one world but could not fully relate to the other."

Today there is a trend toward the re-establishment of outpost camps while houses are retained in settlements such as Pond Inlet — the best of both worlds. A serious question arising from this trend, however, is its impact on wildlife populations. The snowmobile, power-boat, and airplane have sharply changed the rules and have opened up a lot of new territory. One species feeling the pressure is the narwhal.

Late one morning we were walking on the dry slopes above the sea when we heard the unmistakeable "whoosh" of a whale breathing out. Down in the calm waters below, three narwhals, the first of many, swam swiftly by. "But how," I said, "are we going to film these animals? They are usually too far from shore for good photography." Although we desperately wanted to try from a helicopter, the film budget had worn thin, and no helicopters were working near Pond Inlet. A boat, drifting with the engine stopped, might work, but there would be a problem with ice and wind, and the moment the engine started up the whales would dive. We decided we would set up long lenses on a rocky point, several kilometres to the east, and hope for the best. However, we knew that whales filmed at an oblique angle reveal only a fraction of their bodies. We still wanted to get above them.

And then, very conveniently, an opportunity to do just that arrived. In the far distance, something was moving steadily through the floes. Two pairs of binoculars swung up simultaneously, and we knew we might have the answer to our problem — a powerful red and white ship, painted in the colours of the Canadian Coast Guard, was heading toward Pond Inlet. And, as every intelligent film maker knows, ice-breakers carry helicopters.

As we had expected, the ice-breaker, which was Canada's newest and most modern, stopped a few kilometres off shore. Before long, a sleek red and white Jet Ranger rose from its stern and began buzzing toward the air strip, about a fifteen-minute jog from our hotel. I began to jog. By the time I reached the strip, the pilot was busy with some maintenance and waiting for one of the ship's officers, who had come ashore with him. I slowed down and sauntered up to the helicopter, as though vaguely interested in this chunk of machinery that had just dropped in. The pilot, not fooled for a second, waited for the question that he surely knew was coming. Then I had a brain wave. "Would you mind radioing your captain?" I asked. "We're doing some filming here, and we'd really like to include his ship in our film." The answer came back from the ship immediately, with a friendly invitation for lunch. A half-hour later we were in the air and staring down in astonishment at the ice floes.

In groups of a dozen or more, and apparently resting, male narwhals were loafing among the floes, their long tusks visible against the calm water. En route to the ice-breaker, we counted more than forty of them. We landed on the deck in a state of high excitement, still not sure whether our plans to steal the chopper and its pilot were going to succeed, and knowing that it was too soon to ask. We ate lunch with a group of interesting and courteous officers and went on a tour of an immaculate ship, our minds working furiously all the time. Finally, it was time to ask. I turned to the First Officer. "Do you ever let people, ah, use your helicopter?" I asked, hating the way I had phrased the question. "Sometimes, if we feel there is a good reason," he said. "Where do you want to go?" "To film those narwhals," I answered, and we were on our way.

At first we flew high, trying to assess the narwhals' response to the chopper without harassing them. They seemed to ignore us, so the pilot dropped down, bit by bit. Because it is impossible to film with long lenses from a helicopter — there is too much movement — we had to get as close as possible. By now we had counted more than 200, most of them males with tusks. Amazingly, they were not frightened by this whirling, noisy object in the sky, and we were soon shooting from a range of about sixty metres. The trick was to locate a group from a good altitude, and then slip down sideways so that the camera could hold them in view all the way. In less than an hour, we had fifteen minutes of film in the can, all of it good, usable footage. We returned happily to the ice-breaker, filmed a sequence on deck with the chopper coming and going, and then returned to Pond Inlet, grateful for this unique opportunity.

That night we sat on the grey-green lichen-covered boulders in the hills just east of Pond Inlet, watching the ice floes below. The sun dipped low across the north sky, just touching the mountains of Bylot Island and casting an orange glow in the mist above the sea. Telltale lines of gleaming ripples broke the quiet water as little groups of narwhals slipped through the leads and channels in the ice. They did not rise from the depths with a majestic explosion of breath like a bowhead whale, for they were many times smaller, but sometimes we could see their tusks flashing in the arctic sun as they rose and breathed and dived again. They were unforgettable, unicorns in a sea of fire, worthy of all their legends.

Other eyes had spotted the narwhals swimming by in the midnight sun. Soon there was gun-fire over the water. Some hunters went out in boats, pursuing the animals and firing rapidly as they rose to breathe. Bullets slapped the water as hunters tried to herd the narwhals into the shallows. Other hunters stood quietly on ice floes, .303 rifles at the ready. It was not easy to watch. Although the community had a conservative quota of one hundred whales, many more than that would die. A clean kill is only possible when the animal is struck in the brain at just the right angle, slightly downward at fairly close range. No one knows how many wounded whales sink after impact, but a loss rate of one in two is generally accepted as average. Dead females, which have no tusks, often go unreported. Unborn calves die with their mothers, and orphaned calves may die of starvation. When these losses are taken into account, the actual number killed may be two or three times the quota.

Narwhal ivory, which is purchased by the Hudson's Bay Company and by tourists, is a cash crop for Inuit hunters. Each tusk, if it is unbroken, can be worth hundreds of dollars. This has obscured the cultural significance of the hunt and is also causing alarm among scientists. So little has been known about narwhal populations and distributions that it has been difficult to estimate what the quota should be or whether the hunt should be stopped. Unfortunately, the management question cannot be separated cleanly from political and emotional questions, and the whale is the loser. Inuit hunters are sensitive about criticism from the south, and politicians tend to be timid when it comes to game laws in the north. Caught in the middle are the scientists who are trying to find the answers to some basic questions. For example, is the total narwhal population large enough to sustain itself in spite of the hunt, or are more animals being removed than can be replaced by normal reproduction? In particular, how can hunting methods be improved so that fewer animals are "struck but lost?" Beyond these management issues lies a hornet's nest of more emotional issues, which quickly stir up the sometimes uneasy relationships between those who want to make rules and the Inuit who live and hunt in this wild land.

After two long filming expeditions to the High Arctic islands, our sense of wonder for this region remains intact. Although we were working — trying to cope with daunting logistical problems, extremes of weather, large quantities of gear and the day to day imperative of shooting film — we left almost every location with the wish that we could return some day. The Arctic has that effect on visitors, at least in the summer when the climate is usually pleasant, if a little unpredictable. Our most satisfying experiences always came to us when we were alone in wilderness camps, after the Otter had thumped and bumped its way into the air and left us to our own resources for a while. Soon the peace of the land descended over us. Wildlife appeared, weather systems came and went, pressures and urgencies evaporated. In places like these, we had time to record the High Arctic experience, whether it was the arctic hare nibbling and hopping its way into our camp, the changing drama of light and shadow in the mountains, or the ruddy turnstone actually turning over stones beside a glacial creek. Often we lingered over our soup and bannock to contemplate settings as perfect as one might wish for — iridescent blue ice floes drifting along the shore, a stream trickling down through brilliant tundra flowers, and the soft white shades of mountain ice caps and glaciers. Sometimes the wind hammered our little tents mercilessly; sometimes there was only the silence of the Arctic. Rarely did we sleep before midnight, for when the sun dips to its lowest point in the north, the light has a pale, clean beauty touched with shades of gold. It is not surprising that visitors are amazed to discover such scenery in a land usually considered hostile and bleak. And perhaps that is the best part of it — the realization that in this age of instant communication and swift transportation we can still find corners of our world where surprise and wonder are constantly with us.

TRAVELLING AND CAMPING TIPS

WHEN THE RAIN has been finding its way into your tent for three days, and you are choking down a freeze-dried chicken stew that has all the appeal of cardboard boiled in sawdust, your conversation tends to dwell on what went wrong. There is nothing like a little discomfort to focus the mind. When we first started camping around the backwoods of Canada, we made every mistake in the book. But every frozen foot, uncomfortable night, overloaded pack, or inedible meal drove home its own lesson. All we had to do was pay attention, keep notes, and learn from our mistakes.

EQUIPMENT AND FOOD LIST

Before long, we had a well-thumbed notebook with a check-list of tested clothing and equipment that we could use as a basis for planning and packing. We drew the list up about ten years ago, and it is surprising how well it has stood the test of time. It was originally based on an autumn canoe trip in northern Ontario with various extremes of weather anticipated, plenty of portages to negotiate, and a big, windy lake to cross. We can look it over and add or delete items according to the time of year and where we are going. Basically, it is a list of the minimum gear required to keep two people warm, dry and adequately fed for about ten days, regardless of weather. All of the gear has to fit into three packs that will stow neatly between paddlers in a cedar and canvas canoe.

For a trip on Lake Superior, we add a separate box for food, because there is no portaging involved. If we are heading into colder conditions, we take warmer sleeping-bags and heavier clothing.

One large pack contains the following:
1 tent (for 2 people), with poles and pegs
1 nylon fly-sheet, if necessary
2 medium-weight sleeping-bags
2 sleeping pads and/or light air mattresses
2 light outer shells for sleeping-bags, if room. Good for cold conditions.
2 pillow cases (stuff them with spare clothing at night)
2 flashlights, with extra batteries
2 towels and wash-cloths
1 light nylon tarp (for covering gear at night)
Some heavy duty garbage bags

This pack is opened first at the campsite, providing fast shelter in rainy weather, or at the end of a long day. It is the largest and bulkiest pack (ours is the Duluth type) and the least comfortable one to carry. If rough water is anticipated, each item is wrapped inside a strong plastic garbage bag so that the pack is virtually waterproof. It is important to keep the sleeping-bags dry, particularly if they are filled with down.

The rest of the gear is distributed between the two remaining packs. The top compartment of one pack is exactly large enough to accept a box containing the food for an eight-day trip. A cardboard file box, waterproofed with tape and plastic on the outside, is a perfect container, and eliminates the problem of having food scattered among every available pocket and crevice in the packs. Both of these packs have internal frames.

Next is a list of basic clothing for each person:
1 pair of hiking boots, to be kept dry
1 pair of running shoes, for wet conditions in mild weather

1 wool jacket or substantial windbreaker

1 down vest (stuff it in the pillow-case at night)

3 light shirts

Underwear

1 thick wool sweater

2 pairs of jeans

3 pairs of socks

1 complete rain suit (include a nylon poncho for hiking and standing around, if there is room)

1 pair of light gloves

1 waterproof hat

Most of the items listed thus far are basic necessities related to keeping warm and dry and getting a good night's sleep. The tricky part is jamming in all of the other bits and pieces, particularly when camera gear is involved.

The list continues:

15 metres of light nylon rope (it has a million uses)

1 folding saw, with an extra blade

1 set of nesting billy cans

2 plates, mugs, bowls (all of strong plastic)

1 small Teflon frying pan (for bannock)

2 sets knife, fork, spoon

1 roll paper towels

Scouring pad and soap for dishes

1 small spatula

1 small roll of duct tape (good for patching the canoe)

Binoculars

Matches

A few candles and a folding windproof candle holder

Compass

Maps of the area

First aid kit (ask a doctor's advice on what to take)

Small mirror (stainless steel)

Swiss army knife, with most of the attachments

The above lists contain essential items, many of them small and easy to pack. Now we come to the variables — items of personal choice or preference, mostly camera gear in our case. Camera equipment might include:

2 camera bodies and as many lenses as possible

1 small but sturdy tripod

Electronic flash with spare batteries

Filters

Accessories (such as close-up lenses)

Film

Each lens and camera body should be protected inside individual pouches that are foam lined and made of waterproof nylon. A belt loop on each pouch is very handy. A couple of light nylon ski packs, rolled up empty and tied on to one of the main packs, can be used around the campsite and on side-trips to carry the pouches and their contents and to generally keep the camera gear together. Completely waterproof plastic camera cases are available from good outfitting stores.

As to other gear: it is now considered a good environmental practice to carry and use a small stove, instead of making fires. Many popular campsites are actually running out of naturally available firewood, and the surrounding trees have been stripped of lower branches by campers desperate for fuel. A well-designed stove is fast and efficient, and really handy in wet weather. We recommend the type that uses liquid white gas (naphtha) as this fuel is readily available in every tiny corner of the country. Even in the High Arctic, in far-flung Inuit communities, you can always find it.

There is also the question of food. We started with the premise that we were not willing to carry heavy, waterfilled foods in a land so rich in pure water. Better to add the water in camp and keep the food pack as light as possible. A few years of trial and error produced the following menu:

BREAKFAST	*LUNCH*
Oatmeal porridge with raisins	Dried soup and a bannock
Dried milk	Margarine (for the bannock)
Brown sugar	Tea, coffee, or Tang
Tea	

Bannock Recipe

175 mL (3/4 cup) whole wheat flour

125 mL (1/2 cup) Quick Quaker Oats

60 mL (1/4 cup) corn meal

(Proportions of above can vary according to taste; total amount should equal 375 mL [$1^1/_2$ cups])

10 mL (2 heaping tsp) baking powder

1.25 mL (1/4 tsp) salt

a handful of raisins

caraway seeds (amount according to taste)

250 mL (1 cup) water

Mix dry ingredients. Add water and blend into moist dough. Fry with a little oil or shortening over low heat approximately 10 to 15 minutes per side, or until golden brown. Serve hot with butter or margarine.

For convenience on the trail, or when packing food for a canoe trip, mix individual bannocks ahead of time and carry them in separate Zip Lock plastic bags.

SUPPER

Freeze-dried main course	A couple of oatmeal cookies
Freeze-dried vegetable	Hot chocolate, tea, or coffee
Freeze-dried dessert	

Only the sugar, margarine, and cooking oil have any weight to them. Everything else is as dry as dust, except for the raisins in the bannock. If space and weight considerations permit, we carry some extra packets of raisins, two small tins of corned beef (you can make a nice corned beef hash with instant mashed potato), and perhaps a little maple syrup for the bannock. One great advantage of this menu is that there is no smell to the food pack, and this is important in bear country. In addition, there is almost no garbage to bring out. Only the corned beef tins and the unburned foil wrappers from the freeze-dried food envelopes must be retrieved and brought home. Everything else burns up or comes back in a re-usable container.

Our camping list may not be just right for everyone, nor will it be correct for every type of journey. We look upon it as a reminder, something to be consulted for details that might otherwise be forgotten. It is also constantly in danger of being compromised by the addition of luxury items, emergency equipment, extra camera gear, and by the little odds and ends that can creep into the packs one by one. If you start finding tins of smoked oysters squirrelled away in a side pocket of a pack, you can be sure that someone is making unauthorized additions!

If everything is working out as planned, and you are dry, comfortable, and adequately fed, the wilderness experience will be constantly satisfying. When the rain is pouring down and you are sitting under a tightly stretched tarp at the door of a well-pitched tent, sipping hot chocolate, and reading a good book, the many hours of planning will be paying off in the feeling that you can handle with ease a situation that could be wet, miserable, and extremely uncomfortable. This is part of the pleasure of a well-executed canoe trip. That pleasure is sharply reduced by wet boots, sodden sleeping-bags, a leaky tent, and cold people.

CHOOSING A TENT

Most campers can argue endlessly on this subject. All of us have strong opinions and absolute proof that one tent is better than another. However, it is a good idea to seek out experienced campers and ask their advice before you buy. Your choice will be influenced by where you plan to use the tent, and under what conditions of wind and weather. Many people have two or three tents, each one designed for a special purpose.

Tent designs have changed and developed so much in the past few years that choosing a tent for all seasons and all locations has become a bewildering business. Our instinct has always been to keep the design simple. Most light-weight wilderness tents are made of nylon, often in two layers, but some have rather complex designs calling for elaborate pole systems to stretch out the walls. If thin aluminum poles have to be carefully threaded through the material in order to pitch the tent, it may be very difficult to put up and take down in a high wind, with the nylon flapping and trying to sail away. And the loss or breakage of just one aluminum cross-piece can render the entire tent useless. Recently, an Everest expedition lost the use of one of its tents when a climber accidentally stepped on one of the thin tubes and snapped it. A good criterion for buying a tent is this: Can I still pitch it if one of the poles, or pieces, is lost or broken? At least make sure that you carry spare parts, particularly if some of them are small or fragile. And take some strong tape.

We have two tents. Our favourite is an old Black's Strathcona, a simple and traditional design, made of breathable cotton and very easy to pitch. All we have to do is peg out its four corners, raise the aluminum centre pole, and we can start putting in the gear. It is a design that has passed many a test, including gale force winds. The centre pole is very strong, but in an emergency it can be replaced by a stick, or even a paddle. In the High Arctic, where there are no sticks or trees, we carry a spare section for the pole. The only drawback is that this tent, like all cotton tents, requires a separate nylon fly-sheet for heavy rains. Our second tent is a two-person Cannondale, made of nylon, with a built-in fly-sheet. The inner wall is nylon that breathes and the outer wall is coated. Its best feature is a large, protected vestibule where two people can sit, read, and eat in the worst kinds of weather. However, because it is held up by curving sections of aluminum and fibreglass, it is also true that the loss of one section would make the tent almost impossible to pitch. Putting the tent up or taking it down in a high wind also keeps two people rather busy, but if we have to sit out a long storm, this is the tent we choose. For extended filming trips we take both tents. We sleep in the Strathcona and eat and keep gear in the Cannondale.

SPECIAL CONSIDERATIONS FOR DANGEROUS CONDITIONS
The Nahanni

What sets Nahanni apart from most other national parks is the constant element of danger, the real risk for visitors who come to run the river by canoe. The South Nahanni must be treated with great respect; once you slide a canoe into those currents you are committed. There is no paddling back upstream, and only a few places for a float-equipped aircraft to lift you out of trouble. Canoeists uncertain about their skills in white water are well advised to travel in the company of a competent guide, or at least make sure that someone on the trip has plenty of experience, common sense, and leadership ability.

On any long canoe trip, water is always the enemy. It may come in the form of rain, perhaps days of it, but on the South Nahanni it is almost certain to arrive in large quantities from the river itself. Water has a way of always seeking out your sleeping-bag, or the dried milk powder, or the inside of a camera case. There is nothing worse than two weeks in a damp sleeping-bag, or a parade of dazzling scenery going by unrecorded because your camera is full of glacial silt. Because of the considerable chance of canoes being swamped, planning should be done with extra care. The gear that we listed earlier will contain most of the necessary items, but special attention should be given to these below:

CANOE: The canoe should be at least 5 metres long and built wide and deep. Avoid canoes with low, narrow bows or shallow depth. The depth at the centre thwart should be at least 38 centimetres. It should be made of aluminum or heavy plastic. Wally Schaber recommends Royalex for novices on his trips because "they just bounce their way down through the Rock Gardens." The rocks are round and the Royalex absorbs the blows. All canoes should have splash covers for the large standing waves in places like Fourth Canyon. This will prevent un-necessary swamping from waves that curl into the canoe and from the plunging of the canoe as it dives into the trough. Some canoeists prefer not to use their splash covers in the rapids of the Rock Gardens; they would rather be able to get out in a hurry and avoid the danger of entanglement underwater and the chance of serious injury from the rocks. A few paddlers use helmets as a safety measure in these rapids.

PADDLES: An extra paddle in each canoe is essential — a good strong one. Paddles should be wide and well constructed, and it's not a bad idea to fibreglass the tip for added strength.

REPAIR KIT: Each canoe should carry an adequate kit for repairing minor and serious damage. A roll of duct tape, for example, is useful for temporary repairs of small leaks.

ROPE: Take enough floating nylon rope for use as bow and stern lines when tracking along the shore, but keep it secured and out of the way when not in use. There is a real danger from entanglement in a rope if you capsize. One way of keeping rope handy (for holding on to the canoe before it disappears down several kilometres of rapids) is to keep the bow line inside a plastic stuff sack, with one end tied to the canoe. In an emergency, you can grab the bag of rope and unreel it. And floating rope will not wrap itself around your leg underwater.

GENERAL SAFETY: Everyone should carry — in his or her clothing — a waterproof container of "strike anywhere" matches. The tips of these can be waxed for extra protection. All life-jackets should be regulation size and made of non-absorbent material. They will be in constant use. Knee pads are also a good idea, especially for aluminum canoes, which are hard and cold. A piece of Ensolite makes life easier on an aluminum seat. Because of the isolation of this area and the potential for injury, there should be a good repair kit for people in each group of canoeists. The contents of the first aid kit should be thoroughly researched ahead of time, paying attention to any special needs of individuals.

PACKS: Deep packs that can be lined easily with heavy plastic bags are the best. The plastic liner should be much heavier than regular garbage bags, with lots of height so that the top can be folded over several times and then cinched with straps. Fancy hiking packs full of pockets and bristling with aluminum frames should be left at home. Assume that the pack will get submerged and that your sleeping-bag, food, and precious camera gear will be inside. All packing should be done with an eye to wet conditions. The main consideration should be a strategy for packing and stowing gear that will prevent it from being lost or soaked if you dump, and which will permit you to remove the packs easily from a waterlogged canoe. A properly waterproofed pack should float and be recoverable. It is hard enough to empty a canoe in midstream without having to struggle with packs that are saturated and stubbornly lashed in. Bill Mason solves these problems by using the large Duluth type packs, with heavy plastic liners that can be folded over and sealed. After loading the packs into the canoe, he ties a short rope to one thwart, passes it through the straps of each pack, and ties it off on the last pack. In an emergency, only one knot (the last one) has to be untied or cut to free all the packs. When your canoe is full of water and pinned against a rock, and you are struggling to stand upright in a powerful current, getting those packs out of the way quickly is important.

SLEEPING-BAGS FOR WET CONDITIONS: The debate about synthetics versus down goes on. It is largely a matter of personal preference; however, a down bag that gets wet is useless and may take a long time to dry — a procedure that can be complicated by rainy weather. The new synthetics are bulkier, but dry quickly, and will not lose their loft the way that a wet down bag will. On a river trip like this the synthetics make sense. Keep the bag inside its own plastic liner within the pack as an extra measure of safety. As a general rule of thumb consider this scenario. You have just capsized, and all of your packs have been underwater or floating around. You are wet from head to foot. If your planning and packing has been well done, you should now be able to make camp, put on dry clothing, light a fire and cook a meal, and then go to sleep in a warm, dry bag. It may not work out quite that way as water has a knack of finding weak spots, but a scenario like this gives you something to aim for.

Lake Superior
Much of the advice relating to the South Nahanni will apply here. Instead of rapids, however, there will be wind and rough water. Although many people paddle Superior competently and safely, and the voyageurs travelled the shoreline regularly, it is still considered a dangerous lake for canoeing because of the constant possibility of sudden weather changes. Safety should be at the top of the list. It is normal to be windbound one day out of three and the escape route in an emergency may be blocked by stormy conditions. A deep, wide, long canoe with a well-fitted splash cover makes a lot of sense on Lake Superior. And, as mentioned earlier, you are forced to pack carefully in order to fit the cover over the gear. This has another advantage — the canoe presents a very clean and streamlined shape to the wind and is much easier to handle. Remember, too, that canoes will be close to shore and away from most powerboat traffic, so it is a good idea to carry a brightly coloured tarp or even a flare pistol for attracting attention in case of trouble. Above all, make sure that a reliable friend knows where you are going and when you plan to return so that you will be missed if you fail to show up on schedule. Also, find someone who knows the area and can mark up your topographical maps with interesting and useful notes on good camping sites, dangerous headlands, or places to explore. Good research will make any trip far more enjoyable and safe.

A WORD ON THE PHOTOGRAPHS
The photographs were shot on Kodachrome 25 and Kodachrome 64 film, with one exception, on page 27. Ektachrome 200 was used here to assure a high shutter speed while we were shooting from a violently bouncing boat. We prefer fine-grained films for nature photography, and we have found the processing of Kodachrome to be generally reliable, with only a few occurrences of processing errors or damage. Apart from the occasional use of Ektachrome, we have not tried any other colour reversal films, some of which may be excellent.

Four cameras were used: a Leicaflex SL and SL2, a Leica R4, and a Leica M5. Lenses included 24 mm, 28 mm, 35 mm, 60 mm macro, 90 mm, 180 mm, and 400 mm. The Leica R4 has an electric winder, which is useful for aerial photography. We find the precision spot meters in these cameras to be vital for wildlife photography, and for selecting and isolating light readings in scenes with wide variations of colour and light. However, we always carry a Spectra incident meter for settling arguments with the camera in tricky lighting situations and for use with the 16 mm motion picture camera.